SELLING
NEW HOMES

Charles R. Clark and David F. Parker, Clark Parker Associates

D1614114

National Association of Home Builders
15th and M Streets, N.W.
Washington, D.C. 20005

Selling New Homes
ISBN 0-86718-336-5

Library of Congress Cataloging in Publication Data

Clark, Charles R., 1930-
    Selling new homes/Charles R. Clark and David F. Parker.
       p.   cm.
    ISBN 0-86718-336-5 : $22.00 (est.) ($17.60 to NAHB members)
       1. House selling. 2. Real estate business. I. Parker, David
F., 1934-   . II. Title.
    HD1390.5.C573   1989
    333.33'8'0688—dc20

89-34605
CIP

For further information, please contact:
    NAHB Bookstore
    15th and M Streets, N.W.
    Washington, D.C. 20005
    (800) 368-5242

9/89 SCOTT/PORT CITY 3K

Contents

Acknowledgments *page* vi

About the Authors *page* vii

1. Introduction 1

SELL

2. Organizing and Compensating the Sales Team 5
3. Establishing Sales Policies and Procedures 15
4. Hiring and Preparing the Sales Team 49
5. Selling New Homes: The Success Formula 67
6. Implementing a Broker Cooperation Program 95
7. Ensuring Sales Through Purchaser Satisfaction 109

MONITOR

8. Profiting from Consumer Analysis 125
9. Evaluating Sales Performance 135

Appendix A 143

Appendix B 153

Glossary 157

Figures

2. Organizing and Compensating the Sales Team

2-1: Developer/Builder Primary Organization 9
2-2: Subjective Method—Determining Number
        of Salespersons 10
2-3: Budget Method—Determining Number of Salespersons 11
2-4: Sales Office Operating/Supply Checklist 13

3. Establishing Sales Policies and Procedures

3-1: Commission Schedule 18
3-2: Commission Summary Sheet 18
3-3: Termination Form 19
3-4: Individual Sales Goals Form 21
3-5: Competition Selling Evaluation 24
3-6: Weekly Merchandising Checklist 26
3-7: Long Distance Calls Log 28
3-8: Prospect Card 30
3-9: Sample Housing Origin Codes 31
3-10: Sample Housing Source Codes 31
3-11: Daily Sales Activity Form 32
3-12: Purchaser Profile Summary 35
3-13: Sample Purchase and Sales Agreement 37
3-14: Purchaser Information Form 38
3-15: Contract Processing Checklist 39
3-16: Sample Purchaser Letter 40
3-17: Sample New Home Price Breakdown Form 41
3-18: Sample Modifications Form 43
3-19: Sample Selection Sheet 44
3-20: Sample Receipt for Homeowners Association Documents ... 45
3-21: Sample Agreement to Join Homeowners Association 46
3-22: Purchaser Financial Analysis 47
3-23: Purchaser Contact Log 48

4. Hiring and Preparing the Sales Team

4-1: Job Description: Salesperson 51
4-2: Job Description: Sales Director 52
4-3: Sample Recruitment Ads 53
4-4: Resume Evaluation/Rating Form 54
4-5: Sample Interview Questions 56
4-6: Interview Evaluation/Rating Form 57
4-7: Candidate Self-Evaluation 58
4-8: Two-Week Orientation Plan 60
4-9: Sample Letter of Agreement 61
4-10: Sample Compensation Agreement 62
4-11: Consumer Financing Worksheet 64
4-12: The Real Cost of Homeownership 65

5. Selling New Homes: The Success Formula

5-1: Professional Words and Phrases 69
5-2: Specific Non-Verbal Gestures and Their Interpretation 71
5-3: Critical Path to Successful Selling 73
5-4: Qualify for Efficiency 75
5-5: Community Profile Form 76
5-6: Professional Product Demonstration 78
5-7: Ownership Analysis Form 80
5-8: Appointment Potential 82
5-9: Model Dialogue: Incoming Telephone Calls 83
5-10: Model Dialogue: Outgoing Telephone Calls 83
5-11: Sample Personal Note 85
5-12: Sample Envelopes 86
5-13: Common Sales Objections and Suggested Answers 88

6. Implementing a Broker Cooperation Program

6-1: Sample Broker Fact Sheet 104
6-2: Broker Registration Card 105
6-3: Sample Letter Confirming a Broker/Client Registration 106
6-4: Broker Survey 108

7. Ensuring Sales Through Purchaser Satisfaction

7-1: Sample Description: Options and Features 113
7-2: Document Flow Chart 114
7-3: Home Purchaser's Affidavit of Acceptable Completion 118
7-4: Sample Moving Checklist 119

8. Profiting from Consumer Analysis

8-1: Sample Homeowners Survey 128
8-2: Sample Exit Survey 133

9. Evaluating Sales Performance

9-1: Marketing and Sales Performance Evaluation System 136
9-2: Sales Activity Summary 139
9-3: Marketing Response Summary 140
9-4: Sample Marketing Cost-Effectiveness 141

Acknowledgments

Charlie Clark and David Parker dedicate this book to all of the colleagues, critics, clients, and students who have helped us increase our knowledge of this business over the past three decades. More specifically, we extend special thanks to our Vice President, Polly Webb, whose ideas and writing are integrated with our own throughout the book; to Teresa Evans, who typed and coordinated the entire text; and to Ginny Towers, who prepared the glossary. We are grateful also for the comments and contributions of Clark Parker Associates' John King, Lillian Worthington, Cindy Warren, and Barbara Smucygz, as well as our former associate Larry Collins. Special thanks to Briggs Napier Jr., Clark Rector, and Neil Glynn for their review of the initial draft.

At the National Association of Home Builders, our thanks to Susan Bradford, Director of Publications, and to Curt Hane, who edited and coordinated publication of this book. Thanks also to Meg Heck, executive director of the National Sales and Marketing Council.

Finally, but perhaps most importantly, we are grateful for the patience and love of Trudy Clark and Marilynn Parker, who support our dedication and commitment to improving the art and science of marketing and selling new homes.

This book was produced under the general direction of Kent Colton, NAHB Executive Vice President, in association with NAHB staff members James E. Johnson, Jr., Staff Vice President, Operations and Information Services; Adrienne Ash, Assistant Staff Vice President, Publishing Services; and David Rhodes, Art Director.

About the Authors

Charles R. Clark and David F. Parker are the founders and principals of Clark Parker Associates, Inc., an international real estate marketing and sales consultant organization headquartered in Jacksonville, Florida.

Charlie Clark is known by builders, REALTORS®, and lenders throughout the United States and Britain for his educational and motivational seminars on marketing and selling new homes. He is 1989 President of the Institute of Residential Marketing, a founding trustee of the prestigious National Society of Builder Marketing Specialists, Trustee and Vice Chairman of the NAHB Sales and Marketing Council, lecturer for NAHB Regional Leadership Training Conferences, and a featured speaker at the annual conventions of the National Association of Home Builders and the National Association of REALTORS.®

Dr. David Parker has been responsible for a wide range of management, development, and marketing innovations during his career spanning both public and private development of real estate on three continents. He has been a chief executive of development and building companies in addition to serving as planner, researcher, teacher, and consultant. Dr. Parker is the recipient of several design and marketing awards and has authored many articles and reports on marketing, planning, budgeting, and management.

In 1989, Clark and Parker completed *Marketing New Homes* (Washington, D.C.: National Association of Home Builders, 1989), which has received widespread acclaim since its release.

Chapter One

Introduction

Contrary to popular belief, there is no such thing as a born salesperson. Individual selling attributes such as pleasant personality, positive attitude, enthusiasm, self-confidence, and genuine interest in the concerns of other people must be coupled with product knowledge and intensive training and experience in the art and science of selling.

New home salespersons bridge the gap between builder and buyer. This book provides superior techniques for succeeding at the art and science of selling new homes in the following eight chapters organized specifically for home builders and their sales staffs. It is intended to be used as a reference as well as a systematic procedure, with topics organized under headings for ready referral by builders and salespersons.

As the following chapters will emphasize, new home selling must combine appealing presentation with customer-oriented information exchange. The optimum combination of these two elements for a particular product and customer is the art of the successful salesperson. Preparing the buyer with expert knowledge of the builder's product is the science of selling. Builders must therefore strive constantly to create the perfect combination of art and science—the heart of successful sales.

SELL

Chapter Two

Organizing and Compensating the Sales Team

Regardless of size, every builder must sell new homes in order to stay in business. Experience has shown time and again, however, that the alternative of the builder-salesman is often unsatisfactory. Too often, a builder directly involved in a sale must deal with a customer who wants to negotiate price or expects giveaway items—all at the builder's expense. The lack of time and appropriate people skills are other important considerations. While the builder would certainly be wise to become familiar with all aspects of the sales process and stand ready to step in if needed, he or she should concentrate efforts on forming a sales team.

Organizing a New Homes Sales Team

Costs
While cost is obviously a primary consideration when forming a sales team, builders should keep in mind that performance is not necessarily commensurate with price. The costs of a high-quality sales team—be it composed of one dedicated professional or several—can be comparable to those for a mediocre, low-performance team.

Broker or Staff?
The first issue a builder must address when organizing a sales team is whether to enlist a real estate broker to undertake the entire function or to establish an in-house sales team. This age-old broker/in-house-staff issue has become relevant for larger builders as well as small-volume builders in recent years as increasing numbers of real estate firms establish new homes divisions devoted to builder needs. Prior to the emergence of broker specialization in hew homes sales, most real estate agents treated new homes simply as additional listings in their

inventory of consumer offerings rather than as specific products requiring product sales techniques.

The Broker-Builder Gap

The historical gap—between brokers devoted to searching out a suitable residence for a consumer from all available listings and builders devoted to specific product sales—caused a rift of distrust until recent years. This rift has disappeared, or at least substantially diminished, in most market areas as both groups have become more responsive to the interests of the other. While the specifics of builder/broker arrangements designed to expand sales potential are discussed in Chapter Six, "Implementing a Broker Cooperation Program," the following discussion will focus on the pros and cons of outside broker sales management versus an in-house sales team.

The Broker Advantage

The primary advantage of broker sales management is apparent segregation of this often annoying function from daily builder management concerns. Many builders, particularly small-volume builders, believe that turning the entire responsibility (often including all marketing components) over to a broker will allow the builder to concentrate more time and energy on other aspects of the construction business. Unfortunately, adopting this all-too-common attitude is usually a mistake for both parties. Sales activities are integral to all other homebuilding functions and cannot be segregated effectively.

However, a professional real estate broker trained in new homes sales management can become a successful part of the overall management team provided his or her function is integrated with other management functions. Therefore, any builder agreement with a broker must resolve the following three key issues:

Control. The builder must retain full control of the overall sales function while ensuring broker control over sales management. This apparent paradox can be resolved only through strong mutual confidence and excellent builder/broker communication, ensuring that sales are geared entirely toward the builder's products only. This control is similar to the management control that successful builders provide to other key staffpersons, always with the caveat that reporting systems be accurate and frequent and that the builder always retain the right to intercede if problems arise.

Capability. A successful track record in selling new homes is an obvious criterion when selecting a real estate firm. A broker's ability to sell new homes (as distinct from resale homes) can be evaluated by the same criteria used in selecting new employees: training and experience. Some national real estate organizations provide specialized training in new homes sales. In addition, many local real estate brokers are taking advantage of training programs sponsored by professional associations. Builders should insist that all associates assigned to their sales team go through this type of new homes sales training.

Convertibility. An issue of paramount importance, convertibility means converting the builder's prospects to purchase another home (either new or resale) the broker is offering. Of course, the sales team must be totally devoted to selling only the builder's products—no resales and no other builder's products. Many firms still believe it proper for their brokers to meet a prospect attracted to a model home and convert that prospect to purchase another offering on the assumption that they may later reciprocate with a purchaser for one of the builder's homes discovered through another source. Let the builder make no mistake: every prospect inquiring by mail, telephone, or in person is a result of builder marketing expenditures and is therefore the builder's prospect—not the broker's prospect and not eligible to be sold anything else. Every broker should agree to a contractual provision prohibiting convertibility. Any deviation from this no-convertibility rule will dilute the sales program and should not be tolerated.

Getting the Best from Brokers

Of course, the overriding reason to select an outside broker to manage new homes sales is when that broker constitutes the very best available means of selling new homes. In addition to the selection criteria, the following questions for broker candidates should help in determining the best sales management alternative:

- Does the broker have an ongoing sales training program to develop the special new homes sales skills necessary to sell new homes? Is this specialized training conducted prior to the assignment of a salesperson to a site? Is the training continued on a regular and continuing basis throughout the year?
- Does the broker know or care to know every detail of a builder's homes? For example, he or she should be concerned with construction details from foundation to trim, what energy features are included, and why each fixture or feature was selected to provide good service and long-term satisfaction. This product knowledge is essential when demonstrating features and benefits and building perceived value.
- Is the salesperson assigned exclusively to one community or builder? Is he or she permitted to list and sell resale homes or other builder homes? Does the builder have veto power in the selection of this salesperson? In reaching a decision, builders should consider whether they would personally buy a house from this person.
- Is the broker in good standing with the network of cooperative real estate companies through the local Board of REALTORS® and/or a network of relocation systems to attract out-of-town purchasers? These cooperative connections should result in a minimum of 30 percent of sales.

- Is the broker skilled in customer relations on an ongoing basis? Purchaser satisfaction generates referral business that should represent another 30 percent of sales.
- Does the broker have a good track record on the marketing of resale homes (if applicable) in the area? Can the broker offer the possibilities of a trade-in program, whereby the broker guarantees to buy a used house at a specified price over a specified period of time to ensure that a purchaser can commit to a new home?
- Does the broker have a prospect follow-up system after the first contact occurs? Are prospect names managed in an organized fashion from the start?
- Does the broker provide contract administration? Professional contract administration ensures that sale-related documents are prepared directly and circulated properly for efficient and pleasant closings.
- Does the broker provide 24-hour management support? Is the sales team on-call and available to the builder, other salespersons, and purchasers at all times?
- Does the broker schedule a monthly evaluation meeting with the builder to review performance reports and discuss strategies for problem resolution?
- Does the broker follow the principles of organization prescribed by the builder, including a strategic marketing and sales plan and budget, sales policies and procedures, a performance evaluation system providing accurate and timely information about marketing and sales performance, an effective purchaser satisfaction program, and regular monitoring of competitive products and market directions to guide research into potential new business directions?
- Is the broker a member of the National Association of Home Builders (NAHB), the National Sales and Marketing Council, and active in local NAHB activities in the community?

For a complete discussion of broker implementation considerations and techniques, see Chapter Six, "Implementing a Broker Cooperation Program."

Sales Management

As illustrated in Figure 2-1, the overall sales function is interrelated to the other major functions within the builder's organization. Each department or division—finance, planning and design, construction, and marketing and sales—is linked with the others through daily communication and interaction. The builder coordinates these major functions to ensure efficient and profitable results.

Regardless of whether sales management is the responsibility of an outside broker or in-house staff, the builder must ensure that communications flow smoothly between the sales manager or director and other functional managers. Segregation is inefficient and will cause increasing amounts of builder time to correct; integrated teamwork

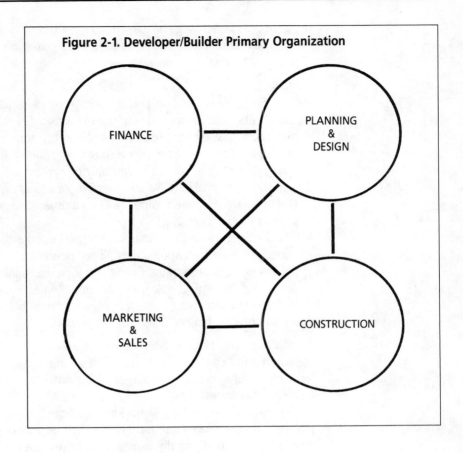

Figure 2-1. Developer/Builder Primary Organization

will generate efficient performance leading to more sales, faster closings, and happy owners who, in turn, will refer new prospects.

Recognizing the importance of overall teamwork, successful builders
ensure balance among their key people. They treat all key personnel
equally and arbitrate normal disagreements between production and
sales personnel with primary attention to the vital continuation of open
communications. Short battles are secondary to the importance of
long-term teamwork.

Although successful teamwork relies upon mutual recognition of
capabilities, each team member will perform best if he or she understands the individual roles of all members of the management team.
This understanding is accomplished best through documented policies
and procedures as described in Chapter Three, "Establishing Sales
Policies and Procedures." Minimizing discretionary decision-making in
any building organization will increase efficiency and make the organization appear more attractive to new recruits.

Organization Strategy

The organization strategy defines the most efficient number of sales
professionals and support staff required for a new community or builder

program. This strategy is based upon competitive and motivational compensation and its relation to projected gross annual revenues.

The number of salespersons is usually determined through one or both of the following methods:

- The Subjective Method relies upon prior experience to determine the number of salespersons and support staff required to greet and present to the estimated number of weekly consumer inquiries and perform follow-up sales processing and reporting activities. Commissions are determined by multiplying typical annual compensation (for the local market) by the number of salespersons and dividing this total by projected annual sales volume to ascertain budget expenditures (Figure 2-2).
- The Budget Method allocates a set percentage of gross sales revenues for sales compensation. This percentage is translated into dollars per sale and multiplied by projected annual sales. The result is divided by typical salesperson annual sales compensation to determine the number of salespersons that can be supported by that community or builder program (Figure 2-3).

In practice, the Budget Method is commonly used to determine the optimum number of salespersons. The result is then considered in the light of experience and modified, along with the budget, to reach a realistic conclusion.

In small-volume selling situations that can support only one salesperson (and therefore cannot meet the desired goal of being open seven days per week), it usually is worthwhile to retain a weekend recep-

---

Figure 2-2. Subjective Method—Determining Number of Salespersons

1. A salesperson following good sales techniques may process 65-70 new inquiries per month. The marketing plan projects an average of 94 new inquiries per month, indicating the need for one salesperson. Since one person cannot adequately "cover" a site, two persons are required.

2. Annual compensation to attract and retain a qualified salesperson in this particular market is estimated to be $40,000 plus insurance and incentive bonuses. Commensurate compensation for a sales director is $60,000, of which $40,000 is salary.

   $40,000 × 2 = $80,000. Plus $30,000 = $110,000.

3. Annual sales are estimated at 30 (average) after initial presales.

   $110,000 divided by 30 = $3667 average compensation/sale.

4. Average sales price is estimated at $230,000.

   $3667 divided by $230,000 = 1.59 percent of sales price plus insurance and incentive bonuses.

Figure 2-3. Budget Method—Determining Number of Salespersons

1. Sales compensation is budgeted at 1.5 percent of gross sales volume.

2. Sales volume is projected to be 30 sales per year, averaging $230,000 per sale.
    30 × $230,000 = $6.90 million.
    $6.90 million × .015 = $103,000 total annual sales compensation.

3. Annual commission to attract and retain two qualified salespersons plus a sales director is estimated at $110,000 plus insurance and incentive bonuses.
    1.5 percent commission generates shortfall of $6,500.

---

tionist to assist the salesperson with traffic surges. In cases in which two salespersons are justified, one should be appointed sales director and paid additional compensation for this dual role.

Salespersons. Effective selling requires concentrated effort and focus that can rarely be achieved by representatives whose attention, loyalties, and income are divided between competing employers. Therefore, successful new homes salespersons are normally full-time employees. They must be experienced, professional, capable of converting prospects into purchasers, and skilled at guiding each transaction to a successful closing. They are the key persons responsible for accurately representing the builder to the public—too important a role for inexperienced or untrained representatives.

Sales Director. The sales director provides professional leadership for planning, directing, and implementing the company's sales policies, strategies, and programs to achieve overall company sales goals. The sales director is a key member of the management team, reporting regularly to other key members and coordinating sales activities with other company activities.

Support Staff. These individuals provide assistance to the sales staff, enabling salespersons to focus on the primary mission of selling. The major support functions are receptionist and secretary (often combined in small operations). The receptionist is ordinarily responsible for visitor comfort when a salesperson is unavailable. The secretary handles office supplies, filing, contract processing, typing, and report preparation.

Compensating a New Home Sales Team

In order to assemble and retain the best possible sales team, compensation must potentially exceed competitive levels and motivate the sales team to top performance. Compensation can be provided in several forms:

- Salary: established salary only is paid on a regular basis.
- Straight commission: compensation of either a flat amount or a percentage of the gross selling price is paid at close of sale.
- Salary plus commission: commission is paid at closing in addition to salary paid on a regular basis.
- Draw or loan against commission: compensation is paid during the selling process, to be settled up against the commission at closing.

Commissions

Commissions motivate salespersons to top performance. However, many builders, particularly those with lengthy pre-sale periods prior to closing, have learned that a "survival" level base salary or draw against commission reduces anxiety and economic stress, focusing the salesperson's full attention on selling. The increasingly popular practice of paying one-half the commission upon a fully approved purchase agreement and the other half at closing can provide a more balanced income stream without removing the commission motivation. Sales director override commissions should be paid on the same schedule as for salespersons.

Other Forms of Compensation

Incentive Bonus Programs. Bonuses above scheduled commissions help sustain productivity at the highest achievable level. Performance incentives should be tied explicitly to planned and budgeted individual sales targets for each quarter. A sales professional should never be rewarded for mediocre performance simply because it exceeds that of colleagues. Conversely, it should be possible for salespersons to achieve incentives by exceeding individual objectives established through prior conferences with the sales director. Sales team objectives in which the entire team, including support staff, share the rewards can also prove useful.

Benefits. Benefits are gaining popularity among salespersons. They obviously have the same health/life insurance concerns as other employees and are attracted and remain loyal to builders who recognize and provide for these concerns.

Facilities, Equipment, and Support

Salespersons perform best when confident of the builder's full support. A high-quality selling environment, with appropriate equipment and supplies to facilitate the selling process, is one sure sign of such support. Figure 2-4 provides a checklist for equipment and supplies to support the sales team. The sales director should define required furnishings, equipment, and supplies appropriate to a specific sales function and plan for storage of sales items in locations convenient to the selling process.

Figure 2-4. Sales Office Operating/Supply Checklist

Sales Office:

Remodeling/Furniture
Equipment
Supplies
Cleaning
Rekeying locks (office/models)
Security system
Power
Telephone
Lighting
Landscaping
Plant maintenance
Music
Sanitary service
Water service

Maintenance:

Maid (per budget)
Exterior (per budget)
Dumpster
Landscaping (per budget)
Irrigation (on timer)

Furniture and Equipment:

Secretary desk
Steno chair
Salesperson desks/tables
Sales chairs
Sales office lighting (lamps)
Bench(es)
Planters
Refrigerator
File cabinet(s)
Typewriter
Water cooler
Tape calculator (print out)
Photocopy machine
Instant camera

Personnel:

Sales director
Salespersons
Receptionist/secretary
Maid (per budget)
Maintenance (exterior, per budget)
Security

Administration:

Sales manuals
Office manual
Petty cash fund
Office supplies account
Printer account
Invoice procedure
Contract processing procedures
File system
Marketing data procedures
Insurance coverage
Subscriptions to print media
Chamber of Commerce membership

Office Supplies:

Stationery
Envelopes (letter and legal)
Postage stamps (commemoratives)
Combination date stamp
Stamp pads
Carbon paper (regular and legal)
Pencils (6 boxes)
Felt pens (2 boxes, green)
Ballpoint pens (box, black)
5 × 7 scratch paper
Petty cash box with lift-out tray
Petty cash receipt slips
Push pins
Rulers
Pencil sharpener(s)
Postage scales
Ashtrays
Wastepaper baskets
Three-hole punch
Three-ring binders
Sets of three-ring dividers
Fasteners
Fastener punch
Legal-size lined tablets (yellow)
Scissors
Letter trays
Rubber bands (box)
Paper clip holders
Staplers
Staples (box)
Tape dispenser
Tape—transparent and double-faced
Staple removers
Telephone message book (duplicate)
Hanging files (legal, one box)

Hanging file racks (legal)
Legal manila folders (third-cut)
Manila folder labels
Cash receipt book
Salesperson's black box (one each)
Card guides—5 × 8
Multi-ring organizers

Household:

Coffee (service)
Sodas (3 dozen, mixed, diet and regular)
Cookies (10 packages with trays)
Candy (hard, individually wrapped)
Glass canisters (3 large, 3 small)
Napkins
Plastic spoons
Cleaner
Bar soap
Toilet tissue
Sponges
Paper towels
Plastic trash bags (slip baskets)
Plastic trash bags ("leaf"-size)
Broom
Door mats
Window cleaner
Furniture polish
Cleaning cloths

Sales Aids:

Brochures
Rack brochures
Price lists
Work sheets (financial)
Floor plans
Reprints (P.R.)
Business cards
Community profile
CPM system forms

Legals:

Purchase and sales agreements/reservation forms
Mortgage applications
Homeowner/condo documents (where applicable)
Escrow account

Chapter Three

Establishing Sales Policies and Procedures

Whether sales are the responsibility of an outside broker or in-house staff, it is equally important that sales policies and procedures be documented in conjunction with—and to the satisfaction of—the builder. This chapter will outline in detail the policies and procedures to include in a sales manual.

Sales Manual Objectives

The purpose of a sales manual is to define all company policies and procedures that guide the sales team toward achievement of builder and individual objectives. By providing written policies and procedures, the builder develops appropriate expectations between employees and management. In addition, written policies instruct new salespersons and help them settle in to new responsibilities. They also provide performance standards by which employees can be evaluated and measured.

A sales policies and procedures manual includes two major sections. The *Organization* section contains policies on the following:

- general management
- administration
- personnel
- compensation
- general accounting procedures
- cooperation

The *Operations* section describes policies on the following:

- sales staff responsibilities
- orientation and education
- model home and sales office procedures

- Prospect Control System
- required sales reporting
- purchaser documents processing and satisfaction.

Organization

The *Organization* section of the sales manual should contain brief, concise text and accompanying exhibits to describe the overall builder organization and the sales organization in particular.

General Management

This section of the manual is usually accompanied by an organization chart and/or a list of key staff and positions. The accompanying text should list the primary company objectives. These objectives might include the following:

- The maintenance and enhancement of a reputation for lasting quality and value.
- Emphasis on the company's commitment to sensitive planning, responsive design, and excellent workmanship as the underlying basis of consumer value.
- Enhancement of the commitment to a policy of service.

This section should describe the means of policy coordination, such as regularly scheduled meetings of builder and key staff in addition to informal communication among these persons to coordinate the major functions of planning and design, financing, construction, marketing, and sales.

Administration

Administration of the sales staff includes the following functions:

- Personnel recruitment, retention, and discharge. The sales director is responsible for all sales and support staff personnel decisions, for achieving sales objectives, and for maintaining individual performance standards.
- Training programs, both in-house and more formal orientation seminars by recognized experts.
- Performance criteria and evaluation for both team and individual production.
- Contract processing of all purchase and sale agreements by salespersons.
- Inventory control of new homes, including speculative homes, contract sales, models, and homesites.
- Interpretation and modification of—as well as staff adherence to—all sales policies and procedures.
- Sales management, including prospect "take-overs" and responsibility for administration of support staff, clerical priorities, files,

supplies, and equipment, subject to budget and accounting coordination.

● Pricing, as established by the builder or chief executive in consultation with the sales director and other key personnel. Old price lists must be destroyed upon receipt of new prices, which are subject to change at any time

Personnel

The sales manual should state clearly that all employees are employed by and are directly responsible to the builder's company, regardless of their possible independent contractor status. All should be expected to read the manual within one week of joining the organization and to abide by the stated policies and procedures.

All salespersons must be licensed by the state prior to beginning work and must sign an employment agreement and job description identifying their relationship with the company. Examples of agreements and job descriptions are provided in Chapter Four, "Hiring and Preparing the Sales Team."

Personnel policies should include specific company rules on sick leave and personal time as well as vacation time and holidays. It should also include authorization and scheduling procedures for absence time.

Compensation

As mentioned earlier, compensation must be based on the principle of attracting and retaining superior professional new homes salespersons. This section of the manual should contain directions on all those issues affecting compensation covered in Chapter Two, including sales commissions/draws against earnings, incentive bonus programs, and benefits.

General Accounting Procedures

At the initiation of each transaction, the salesperson must complete a commission schedule (Figure 3-1), which is attached to the transaction documents and submitted to the sales director or builder with the contract. This form identifies compensation for the salesperson(s) and possible interests of others who may be involved in the transaction. The accounting department or bookkeeper receives this form as authorization for disbursement of commissions upon close of escrow.

Accounting procedures must also include those for recording draws and advances (Figure 3-2) and other reports provided by the company to record both individual commission transactions as well as year-end statements of earnings.

Commission Arbitrations. Arbitrations should be avoided whenever possible by encouraging salespersons to resolve their commission disputes among themselves. When arbitration is necessary, the sales director provides the final decision. In the face of a disputed broker

Figure 3-1. Commission Schedule

Date: _____ Sales Price: _____

Buyer's Name: _____

Address: _____

Salesperson: _____

Bonus: _____

Broker (check one):   Yes _____   No _____

Broker Name and Address: _____

_____

Associate's Name: _____

Amount Due Broker: _____

Bonus (if applicable): _____

Other (please describe): _____

_____

Figure 3-2. Commission Summary Sheet

Name: _____

Month: _____

Total commissions on closings this month: $ _____

Less total draws this month: _____

Previous draw balance: _____

= Total amount due this month: $ _____

= Total amount owed this month: _____

Monthly Summary of Activity

Draws: Closings:

_____   _____

_____   _____

_____   _____

_____   _____

_____   _____

_____   _____

commission, the company should use the arbitration procedures of the local Board of REALTORS®.

Termination and Compensation Agreements. A commission is not fully earned until the sale has closed. Therefore, these documents should provide for the company to retain one-half of all commissions for completion of sales not closed upon an employee's termination. The salesperson must complete a termination form (Figure 3-3). In addition, all company supplies and documents, all transaction files and their contents, and all prospect and purchaser information must remain the sole property of the company in the event of termination.

Reimbursable Expenses. Expenses should never be authorized for salespersons without the approval of the sales director or builder. Procedures for such approval and reimbursement procedures should

---

Figure 3-3. Termination Form

Sales Associate _____ Date _____

Community Assignment _____

Sales Director _____

UPON MY TERMINATION I HAVE THE FOLLOWING PROPERTIES IN ESCROW SUBJECT TO RECORDING. I AM AWARE THESE ESCROWS WILL HAVE TO BE CLOSED BY AN ASSOCIATE OTHER THAN MYSELF. I AGREE TO RELINQUISH 50 PERCENT OF MY COMMISSIONS TO THE COMPANY TO COMPENSATE THE AGENT. I AGREE THAT THE COMMISSION STATED BELOW WILL BE THE PORTION THAT I WILL RECEIVE OF THE TOTAL COMMISSIONS ORIGINALLY INDICATED.

Lot No.	Purchaser	Date Sold	Date Estimated Closing	Adjusted Commission Due At Close	Amount Available to Management for Use with Other Associates

The following items are being returned to the Company:

_____

_____

The information above has been reviewed and agreed to as indicated by the parties whose signatures are affixed below:

_____   _____
Sales Director   (Date)   Sales Associate   (Date)

be set forth in the manual and may include the submission of cash receipts with all check requests.

Return and Forfeiture of Deposits. The sales manual should stress that all such transactions must be minimized. When cancellations cannot be avoided, this section should describe the company's policy with respect to deposit funds. The company decision on deposit retention generally is based on direct and indirect costs resulting from the cancelled transaction, with the salesperson receiving no compensation from such forfeitures. Purchasers should be advised of the company policy on forfeiture of deposits and prepaid charges at the time the purchase agreement is completed. See Chapter Seven, "Ensuring Sales Through Purchaser Satisfaction," for further information on handling purchaser cancellations.

Cooperation

This includes both broker cooperation and cooperation among in-house salespersons. This section of the manual should contain policies and procedures for broker cooperation that encourage and facilitate such sales. In-house cooperation usually is encouraged without commission splitting. If the company has separate sales forces for several distinct communities, inter-community referrals should result in a "referral commission" to the originating associate. This referral fee usually is paid by the company and represents a small reward for taking the time to refer prospects to another community that better suits the prospect's housing budget or needs.

Operations

Operations policies and procedures are intended as general working agreements to provide optimum conditions for individual and team performance. They are subject to modification in accordance with changing needs and requirements.

Sales Staff Responsibilities

These responsibilities include both individual and team sales objectives and staffing assignments. Sales performance standards are best established according to individual goals developed for each salesperson in consultation with the sales director or builder on an annual or semi-annual basis. Figure 3-4 illustrates a summary format for recording individual sales goals. Of course, this section of the manual must also include a statement on conformance to applicable state laws and regulations.

Figure 3-4. Individual Sales Goals Form

NAME: _____ COMMUNITY: _____

During the twelve month period beginning _____ and ending _____ ,
my individual sales goals are as follows:

A. **Total Commission Income:** $ _____

   1. Average commission per home: $ _____

   2. Number of homes to be sold: _____

   3. Conversion ratio: _____

   4. Number of prospects to be contacted: _____

B. **Quarterly Commission Income:** $ _____

   1. Number of homes to be sold: _____

   2. Number of prospects to be contacted: _____

C. **Monthly Commission Income:** $ _____

   1. Number of homes to be sold: _____

   2. Number of prospects to be contacted: _____

D. **Weekly Commission Income:** $ _____

   1. Number of homes to be sold: _____

   2. Number of prospects to be contacted: _____

E. **Daily Commission Income:** $ _____

   1. Number of homes to be sold: _____

   2. Number of prospects to be contacted: _____

_____   _____
     Date   Salesperson

F. **Results:** _____
            Date

	Prospects	Sales	Commission
Goal	_____	_____	_____
Actual	_____	_____	_____
Difference	_____	_____	_____

General Responsibilities. This section should set out general responsibilities of the sales team. For example:

- Personal appearance and the office environment must be neat and organized at all times. The same standard applies to automobiles parked adjacent to the sales office or used in the sales process.
- The salesperson's first responsibility is to sell homes to visitors. This function takes precedence over all other office activities.
- The second responsibility is to maintain clear and complete prospect reports. Every visitor to a community represents expenditure of hundreds of thousands of dollars in land, development, construction, marketing, and merchandising.
- The third responsibility (when not occupied by the above) is telephone re-contact and follow-up with prospects, brokers, and others. Few sales are made without follow-up, and many sales are lost through inattention.
- A final responsibility is knowledge of company homes, the community, and the competition. A prospect expects the salesperson to know every detail of construction methods, design, financing, and the surrounding area.

Sales Staff Appearance and Conduct. In view of the preceding priorities, salespersons should be available at all times unless with a prospect or out of the office by assignment of the sales director. Salespersons will find themselves best prepared if provided with guidelines such as the following:

- Dress and conduct should be appropriate to a business office. The public is not only prospective purchasers, but other builders, bankers, contractors, and industry colleagues. To all of these groups, "the salesperson is the company." Courtesy and good manners toward every visitor should guide specific behavior. For example, it is a breach of courtesy not to stand and greet all visitors.
- How salespersons present themselves will determine personal success as well as public perception of the builder and the company. A new home is the highest-priced item most customers have ever purchased, so sales appearance should fit the image of the homes.
- Men may wear sports jackets or suits. A coat and tie must always be worn. Saleswomen should dress in a conservative and attractive manner—suits, professional-looking dresses, or skirts are required. When site conditions warrant, the sales director may make an exception to this dress code.
- Consumption of alcoholic beverages is prohibited at all times. Smoking should be kept to a minimum in office areas and is prohibited in model homes and the information center display area. Ashtrays should be cleaned immediately after use and stored out of sight. No smoking is permitted when customers are present anywhere in the models or offices.

- A salesperson shall have no authority to bind or obligate the company through any representation unless specifically authorized to do so by senior company personnel in a particular transaction.
- Salespersons are not authorized to refer business to any subcontractor, supplier, or third-party enterprise unless specifically authorized by the company in writing. Salespersons cannot accept fees or gratuities from subcontractors, suppliers, or related business people. Failure to adhere to this policy is cause for immediate dismissal.
- With regard to homeowners insurance, salespersons should advise purchasers to consult friends and associates and contact several different insurance agencies. Salespersons should not recommend any insurance agency or agent specifically. Directing business to a particular firm or individual is interpreted as unfair by many of those with whom a building company does business daily. Doing so can jeopardize a builder's image and reputation.

This section of the sales manual should also detail salespersons' ongoing responsibility to know what properties are for sale and the details of development status relevant to making a sales presentation. Management must supply inventory reports to identify plans and prices for each dwelling or homesite on the market. Each of these updates must have an effective date and be filed immediately as a permanent record of price changes. However, a price list should never be handed out to prospects. A much more effective method involves noting the current price directly on the brochure insert displaying a particular plan, often with the addition of a date and special color to signify urgency.

Finally, this section of the manual might include a request for salespersons' suggestions and recommendations. Instructions should be included detailing procedures for submitting such ideas and how they will be evaluated and initiated.

Orientation and Education
These steps should be mandatory for a sales team's professional growth and development. Builders usually require that all new sales employees participate in company orientation and educational programs. A program for sales training and education during the orientation process should include the following elements:

- Sales policies and procedures manual should be required reading during the first week on the job, establishing the framework for the balance of the orientation.
- New salespersons should be teamed with an experienced colleague whenever possible for a two- to four-week observation period. The experienced employee should be willing to answer questions, demonstrate sales and presentation techniques, evaluate performance, and counsel the new salesperson.

- A planned presentation should be prepared for the new salesperson, usually in conjunction with the sales director after observing experienced salespersons, attending new home sales training, and preparing background information on product, financing, community, and competition.

For further information on orientation and education, see Chapter Four, "Hiring and Preparing the Sales Team."

Community knowledge is essential to the sales process. The sales manual should include checklists for features and benefits of the product offerings; the community in which the product is being offered; and

---

Figure 3-5. Competition Selling Evaluation

Shopper _____ Date _____

Development
Name _____ Developer _____

Address _____

Type of Development

_____ Single-family detached, large lot

_____ Small lot/zero lot line detached

_____ Attached

_____ Multi-level   Number of stories _____

_____ Resort

Location Feature (e.g., riverfront, heavily wooded, etc.) _____
_____

Planned Number of Dwellings in Current Phase _____

Phase # _____

Product or Model:

	# BR/BA	Base Price	Square Footage	Price/Sq. Ft.
1.				
2.				
3.				
4.				

Price Range (low to high) $ _____ to $ _____

Site Amenities (e.g. pool, tennis, etc.) _____

Car Parking (circle)

Outside   Single Garage   Structure Parking

Carport   Double Garage

Dwelling Features (special standard features) _____
_____

(special optional features available) _____
_____

the surrounding area, including its employment, shopping, schools, recreation, and transportation.

Salespersons should also be asked to become fully familiar with competitive products and developments in the surrounding market area. This knowledge is necessary to establish perceived value differences during the sales process. Figure 3-5 illustrates a competition selling evaluation report for analysis of competitive developments.

Model Home and Sales Office Procedures

These procedures control the appearance of the sales office and the product offering. Years of experience have shown that the weekly sales rate is directly affected by the appearance and total presentation of the sales office, models, and production homes. These areas have been developed for customers and selling. Prospective purchasers should never be directed to a company office reserved for administrative functions.

Sales Office Procedures. The entire sales environment should be clean and uncluttered. Specifically:

- Desks should be clear, ashtrays empty, brochures and other materials neat.
- Music, if available, should be at background volume and chosen for a broad range of tastes.
- Salespersons' lunches should not leave a noticeable odor.
- Soft drinks should be provided for customers only. Fresh coffee, brewed at frequent intervals, should be available for both staff and customers.

Figure 3-6 illustrates a weekly merchandising checklist summarizing maintenance responsibilities for sales areas in order to keep them clean and well organized for optimum prospect presentation. For example, pillows, pictures, and furniture in models should be straightened. In addition, draperies in models should be kept open so that homes are filled with light and the landscaping can be viewed from inside.

This section of the sales manual should also include sales office hours, which may vary by community and season but are normally from 11:00 A.M. to dusk Monday through Saturday and noon to dusk on Sunday, or later by appointment. It is vital that the information center and models be ready for viewing during the listed hours.

Telephone Procedures. Telephone manner—and manners—are part of the total impression a builder makes on a community and should be stressed in the manual. The sales team should be instructed to stand out from the rest through the cheerful, warm reception they provide on the telephone. Regardless of who answers the phone, the opening phrase should be upbeat: for example, "It's a beautiful day at (community name or builder)."

Figure 3-6. Weekly Merchandising Checklist

Community: _____

Week Ended: _____

Model Area	Model	Model	Model	Model	Model
1. Are flags free from tears?	____	____	____	____	____
2. Grass cut, well manicured?	____	____	____	____	____
3. Gardens cultivated, weeded?	____	____	____	____	____
4. Stepping stones firm, no cracks to catch heels?	____	____	____	____	____
5. Grounds free of papers, cigarette butts?	____	____	____	____	____
6. Site signs clear, fresh-looking, and upright?	____	____	____	____	____
7. Approach and entry way manicured?	____	____	____	____	____
8. Parkways free of weeds, neat?	____	____	____	____	____
9. Grass fresh, new—not burned out?	____	____	____	____	____
10. Asphalt driveways free of heel marks, clean?	____	____	____	____	____

Model Product

	Model	Model	Model	Model	Model
1. Entry tile clean or carpet clean?	____	____	____	____	____
2. Wallpaper free from peeling?	____	____	____	____	____
3. Carpets free of dirt, scuff marks? Can you call it clean?	____	____	____	____	____
4. *All* lamps working?	____	____	____	____	____
5. Drapes hanging neatly, clean, shirred in corners?	____	____	____	____	____
6. Cigarette butts inside, ashtrays clean?	____	____	____	____	____
7. Pillows neat on chairs, sofas, beds?	____	____	____	____	____
8. Have you reported obvious pilferage for replacement?	____	____	____	____	____
9. Beds made well, bedspreads free of wrinkles?	____	____	____	____	____
10. Toilets clean?	____	____	____	____	____
11. Closets free of debris, storage items?	____	____	____	____	____
12. Unit free of musty, close feeling?	____	____	____	____	____
13. Unit free of odors?	____	____	____	____	____
14. Bathroom scoured, free of dust?	____	____	____	____	____
15. All labels and tags off kitchen and bath fixtures, furniture?	____	____	____	____	____
16. Walls free of dirt?	____	____	____	____	____
17. All doors, cabinets, sliding doors work easily?	____	____	____	____	____
18. Floor tile tightly in place, matched?	____	____	____	____	____
19. All windows, doors, glass, and mirrored surfaces spotlessly clean?	____	____	____	____	____

Figure 3-6. Weekly Merchandising Checklist (continued)

	Model	Model	Model	Model	Model
20. Accessories in place, pictures hung even and straight?	____	____	____	____	____
21. Heater closet free of debris?	____	____	____	____	____
22. Knobs on all drawers, cabinet doors, etc.?	____	____	____	____	____
23. All disclaimers and option stickers in place?	____	____	____	____	____

Sales Office

	Model	Model	Model	Model	Model
1. Desks clear of random papers?	____	____	____	____	____
2. Purchase and sales agreement package on each desk?	____	____	____	____	____
3. Ashtrays clean?	____	____	____	____	____
4. Brochures in neat pile on collecting table?	____	____	____	____	____
5. Only brochures, important collateral on collecting table, nothing else?	____	____	____	____	____
6. Water cooler area clean?	____	____	____	____	____
7. Carpet clean?	____	____	____	____	____
8. Displays hung evenly and straight?	____	____	____	____	____
9. Glass doors clean?	____	____	____	____	____
10. If you serve coffee, are cups clean, serving area spotless, coffee fresh?	____	____	____	____	____
11. Have you removed all random clippings from wall except in approved areas?	____	____	____	____	____
12. Drapes hanging neatly, clean?	____	____	____	____	____
13. Site plan up to date?	____	____	____	____	____
14. Vinyl floor clear of scuffs, waxed?	____	____	____	____	____
15. Are warranties, move-in kits, maintenance booklets out of sight but handy to give to customer?	____	____	____	____	____
16. Have you made complete individual file folder for each lot?	____	____	____	____	____
17. All pertinent documents handy for quick write-up?	____	____	____	____	____
18. Desk drawers clean?	____	____	____	____	____
19. File clear of extraneous material, clean?	____	____	____	____	____

Sales Director _____   Sales Associate _____
                              Signature   Signature

Long distance business calls should be entered on a register (Figure 3-7) and given to the supervisor weekly. Personal calls should be kept to a strict minimum and charged to the originator if long distance.

House Files. Salespersons should be instructed that all files and documents relating to a prospect, a pending sale, a completed sale, or a cancelled sale are the sole property of the company and may not be removed from the office at any time without the express permission of management. All personal information contained in a purchaser file is presumed to be confidential and should be treated accordingly.

Miscellaneous Procedures

Prospect Assignments. Procedures should be included in this section on assignment of prospects to salespersons on an equitable basis in those offices containing more than one salesperson. For instance, it is common to have an "up" system, whereby each salesperson alternates on each inquiry, whether a walk-in, telephone call, or mail response. By rotating these inquiries among the sales force, everyone has a fair and equitable opportunity for selling.

Inventory Control. An inventory control procedure should be established for sales literature and office supplies to ensure adequate supplies are available in advance for all operations. Many successful sales offices provide a "sales professional organizer" for maintaining all rel-

Figure 3-7. Long Distance Calls Log

Date	Prospect's Name	City Called	Phone Number	Caller

evant selling information for easy reference—usually a three-ring binder (often customized with the community or builder name on the cover). The salesperson should carry this organizer during the selling process, referring to its major sections:

- Area
- Community
- Products
- Closing Documents
- Builder History
- Financing

Prospect Control System

The Prospect Control System provides a secure means of recording initial and continuing relationships with prospects. Prospect cards (Figure 3-8) are filed for each day and month, establishing basic contact objectives. The information on each card constitutes research to understand the problems of selling to that particular prospect. Alternate solutions for achieving appointments and sales should be formulated at the beginning of each day. This preparation is followed by a program of prospect contacts throughout the day. Properly organized, this system provides the basis for individual and team sales success as well as information for performance evaluation of all marketing and sales activities.

Prospect Cards. Each salesperson's sales reporting and follow-up emanate from the prospect cards. Salespersons must complete these cards for each and every prospect immediately after initial and follow-up contact. Prospect cards are filed in the salesperson's prospect control file according to month of planned contact and—for the current month—day of planned contact. In a high-traffic office, the secretary or receptionist maintains a duplicate set of prospect cards. This master file is alphabetical and is used as a reference when visitors return to ensure they are reassigned to the salesperson who worked with them on earlier visits.

Origin and Source. Every prospect must be coded according to origin and source (marketing media code for how the prospect learned of the development). Additionally, it should be noted whether the contact was made by mail, telephone, or site visit and whether the prospect is ready, willing, and able (RWA) to purchase. Figures 3-9 and 3-10 provide sample codes for use with sales reporting forms.

Required Sales Reporting

A builder needs daily records to adjust marketing strategies and budgets in support of the sales effort. Figure 3-11 illustrates a daily sales activity form used to extract information from prospect cards and

Figure 3-8. Prospect Card

PROSPECT CARD

PROSPECT
Mr.   Mrs.   Miss   Ms.

COMMUNITY:_____ FIRST CONTACT _____ / /

LOCAL ADDRESS   NON-LOCAL ADDRESS   DAY   DATE

Street			Street		
City	State	Zip	City	State	Zip
H. Phone	B. Phone		H. Phone	B. Phone	

NO. OF PERSONS TO RESIDE   NO. OF BEDROOMS   PRICE RANGE   OCCUPANCY DATE

| | | 1 | 2 | 3 | 4 | $_____ | | | | |

GRADE	FOLLOW-UP NOTES_____
	_____
COOPERATIVE BROKER;	ASSOCIATE
SOURCE	SALES ASSOCIATE

● CLARK PARKER FORM 10

GRADE	CONTACT DATE	CALL BACK DATE	APPOINTMENT		FOLLOW-UP NOTES
			DATE	TIME	

● CLARK PARKER FORM 11

30

record it—either by computer or by hand—for weekly or monthly summarization and analysis:

- Prospect names: recorded for every contact achieved that day.
- New inquiries: recorded according to origin and source, as well as the contact communication medium and the prospect grade (RWA). Other statistics provide important personal evaluation information (for example, percentage of referrals received from previous owners, prospects, and other contacts). Daily totals for all new inquiries are recorded at the bottom of the page.

Figure 3-9. Sample Housing Origin Codes

Origin

DB:	Duval Beaches	DS:	Duval/South
PV:	Ponte Vedra	DW:	Duval/West
DA:	Duval/Arlington	FL:	Other areas in Florida
DN:	Duval/North	US:	Areas outside of Florida in the U.S.

Figure 3-10. Sample Housing Source Codes

Source Codes:	Inquiries Resulting from:	Definition:
OS	Outdoor sign	• Any outdoor sign, be it billboard, poster, or entry sign
NP	Newspaper	• Any newspaper advertisement
MG	Magazine	• Any magazine advertisement
DM	Direct Mail	• Mail sent out to prospective purchasers through an organized print campaign (not salesperson follow-up or prospecting letters)
PO	Promotion	• Any event having directly attributable costs (grand opening, broker party)
TR	Television/Radio	• Television or radio advertising
PR	Publicity	• Public relations articles in newspapers, etc.
RF	Referral	• Personal, friend, relative, acquaintance, or repeat purchaser
AR	Agent Referral	• Real estate broker referral for which a commission or referral fee is normally paid
SP	Self-Prospecting	• Inquiries generated by the efforts of individual salespersons not associated with above activities

Figure 3-11. Daily Sales Activity Form

DAILY SALES ACTIVITY

Community _____
Sales Associate _____
Date _____ Time In _____ Time Out _____
Weather _____
Total Visitor Units _____

NEW INQUIRIES	ORIGIN CODE	SOURCE CODE	Circle Letters in Appropriate Categories			NEW APPT DATE/TIME	SALES ($)	SELL TIME (MIN)
			CONTACT Site Tel. Mail	QUALITY Ready Willing Able				
NAME			S T M	R W A				
			S T M	R W A				
			S T M	R W A				
			S T M	R W A				
			S T M	R W A				
			S T M	R W A				
			S T M	R W A				
			S T M	R W A				
			S T M	R W A				
			S T M	R W A				
			S T M	R W A				
			S T M	R W A				
			S T M	R W A				
			S M	R W A				
PAGE TOTALS							$	

BE-BACKS				QUALITY Ready Willing Able		SALES ($)	CANCELLATIONS ($)	
				R W A				
				R W A				
				R W A				
				R W A				
				R W A				
				R W A				
				R W A				
PAGE TOTALS						$		

32

Figure 3-11. Daily Sales Activity Form, continued

FOLLOW-UPS	CONTACT Person Tel. Mail	QUALITY Ready Willing Able	APPOINTMENT DATE/TIME
NAME			
	P T M	R W A	
	P T M	R W A	
	P T M	R W A	
	P T M	R W A	
	P T M	R W A	
	P T M	R W A	
	P T M	R W A	
	P T M	R W A	
	P T M	R W A	
	P T M	R W A	
	P T M	R W A	
	P T M	R W A	
	P T M	R W A	
	P T M	R W A	
	P T M	R W A	
PAGE TOTALS			
PROSPECTING			
NAME			
	P T M	R W A	
	P T M	R W A	
	P T M	R W A	
	P T M	R W A	
	P T M	R W A	
	P T M	R W A	
	P T M	R W A	
	P T M	R W A	
	P T M	R W A	
	P T M	R W A	
	P T M	R W A	
	P T M	R W A	
PAGE TOTALS			

- Be-backs: graded as those ready, willing, and able to purchase. Be-backs constitute the salesperson's highest-priority prospects—only one in 100 prospects is likely to purchase on the first visit, whereas one in ten is likely to purchase on the second visit, and one in five on the third.
- Follow-up contacts: essential with every new inquiry. Be-back must be achieved in person or by telephone within 48 hours. Mail follow-up is supplementary for confirming oral information. Unsuccessful contact attempts should not be recorded on the summary. Total daily follow-up contacts are recorded at the bottom of the page.
- Prospecting: essential to generating a continuing flow of prospects. Names of contacts and other pertinent information should be provided in the appropriate columns. For more on prospecting, see pp. 85-87.
- New appointments: noted by date on the summary as a cross-check on the prospect card record and to facilitate the next day's activity. Daily total of appointments scheduled is recorded at the bottom of the page.
- Sales agreements and cancellations: listed according to number and dollar volume. Daily totals should indicate the number of sales and cancellations and, at the bottom of the page, the net of sales agreements minus cancellations.
- Selling time (minutes) expended on each prospect: recorded in the right column and totaled at the bottom of the page.

The sales manual must stress that it is the salesperson's responsibility to compile the necessary information on each prospect. Figure 3-12 illustrates a purchaser profile summary that requires specific codes with which every salesperson should quickly become familiar:

- Model: the specific letter/number code or name of model purchased.
- Use: coded as P (primary home), S (secondary home), and I (investment property).
- Source: derived from the daily sales activity source codes.
- Origin: derived from the daily sales activity origin codes.
- Residence type: type of dwelling the purchaser is currently living in, coded as R (rent), D (detached single-family), A (attached; e.g. townhome), C (condominium or multi-family), and M (mobile home).
- Marital status: coded as S (single), M (married), D (divorced), W (widowed), or NMC (non-married couple).
- Head of household age: approximate age of the chief wage earner.
- Head of household income: approximate income in dollars (from the mortgage application).
- Total household income: approximate income in dollars for all wage earners (from the mortgage application).
- Head of household employment: coded in accordance with Standard Industrial Classification—MP (managerial and professional), TS (technical, sales, administrative support), SR (service), LB (labor-

Figure 3-12. Purchaser Profile Summary

PURCHASER PROFILE SUMMARY

Page _____ Of _____

Community: _____
Prepared By: _____
Date of Report: _____
Reporting Period: _____
Sales Director: _____

Signature _____

Purchaser Name	Purchase Price	Model	Type of Sale	Visit Number of Purchase	Use	Previous Residence Type	Type Finan.	Marital Status	Head Hsld. Age	Head Hsld. Income	Total Hsld. Income	Head Hsld. Empl.	Size Family	Children's Ages			Source	Origin
														1-5	5-15	15+		

ers, transport, machine operators), ML (military, active service), RT (retired, not engaged in business).

- Size of family: number of full-time residents and children, coded according to the three age brackets listed at the top of the column.

Purchaser Document Processing and Satisfaction

Satisfied customers are a major source of new sales through referral and repeat business. This final section of the policies and procedures manual should summarize the company's commitment to purchaser satisfaction from the initial consumer contact through ownership and beyond. The following four goals are suggested for achieving purchaser satisfaction:

Goal #1: Appropriate and Mutual Understandings Between the Consumer and Salespersons. This first goal is achieved by ensuring accurate representation of the value and merits of the builder's homes, sales process, and construction process. This is in addition to state and local regulations governing real estate transactions. Misrepresentation—of price, terms, quality, features, benefits, or other factors—by any salesperson should be cause for immediate dismissal.

Goal #2: Clear Written Agreements. This goal requires that all contracts, selection orders, change orders, and contract addenda be complete and accurate. All agreements with the purchaser must be in writing in language that can be understood by the consumer, the builder, and construction personnel. Any questions about contracts should be resolved on a priority basis before a purchase agreement (Figure 3-13) is written. To facilitate collection of purchaser profile information, many salespersons prefer to complete a purchaser information form (Figure 3-14) immediately after the purchase agreement is completed.

Goal #3: Timely Processing of All Agreements. This third goal involves efficient management approval of purchase agreements, including the following:

- Purchase and sale agreement: once a purchase agreement is executed, it is submitted within 24 hours together with all checks, monies, and other necessary documents to the central office or the sales director. The contract processing checklist (Figure 3-15) will also be completed and attached to the transmittal package. A form letter (Figure 3-16) is then sent to the purchaser within 48 hours of receipt of an approved purchase agreement.
- Construction options: each product has a list of standard options that may be purchased at the time the contract is executed. This list is issued by the builder or marketing staff and updated periodically. Option selections should be submitted in writing on a new home price breakdown form (Figure 3-17).

Figure 3-13. Sample Purchase and Sales Agreement

Purchase & Sales Agreement

(Name of builder), hereinafter called "SELLER" hereby agrees to sell to _____
_____ , hereinafter called "BUYER," and the "BUYER" hereby agrees to purchase from "SELLER" the following
described property in _____ County, (State) upon the following terms and conditions:

1. LEGAL DESCRIPTION: Lot _____ , Block _____ , Unit _____ .

Street Address _____ Model No _____

2. PURCHASE PRICE TO BE PAID BY BUYER:

(a) Purchase price of land and basic improvements $ _____

(b) Additional equipment or extras

     1 _____ $ _____

     2 _____ $ _____

     3 _____ $ _____

     4 _____ $ _____

TOTAL PURCHASE PRICE OF LAND, IMPROVEMENTS, EQUIPMENT OR EXTRAS $ _____

3. THE TOTAL PURCHASE PRICE SHALL BE PAYABLE AS FOLLOWS:

(a) Earnest money deposit, receipt of which is hereby acknowledged . . . . $ _____

(b) Additional payment on _____ day of _____ , 19 _____ . . . . $ _____

(c) Additional payment due at closing or delivery of possession, whichever is sooner (not including
closing costs or prepaid items of Buyer) . . . . $ _____

(d) Proceeds of conventional loan to be executed by Buyer at closing . . . . $ _____

     TOTAL PURCHASE PRICE . . . . $ _____

     PLUS Buyer to pay closing costs in the sum of . . . . $ _____

     TOTAL TRANSACTION PRICE . . . . $ _____

In addition, Buyer shall pay at closing prepaid items for taxes, hazard insurance, mortgage insurance premium and review fee, and interim interest, if
applicable, in the approximate sum of $ _____ . All closing costs not paid by Buyer shall be paid by Seller. Taxes for the year in which the sale is
closed shall be prorated between Seller and Buyer as of date of closing.

4. FINANCING: Buyer must apply for a _____ year conventional loan in the sum of $ _____ , within five (5) working days, proceeds
of which shall be paid to Seller at time of closing. The responsibility for arranging such loan is assumed by Seller. Buyer shall furnish promptly all information,
and cause to be executed all documents necessary in connection with said loan application. Seller reserves the right to obtain loan for Buyer for thirty (30)
days after buyer is turned down by another lender.

5. FAILURE TO OBTAIN LOAN: In the event said application for loan is not approved by the mortgage lender within _____ days of date
of this contract the earnest money deposit shall be refunded to Buyer, less credit report charges, appraisal fee, rental charges and damage to house, if any,
and this contract will be null and void.

6. COMPLETION DATE: Seller agrees to complete the proposed construction in accordance with plans and specifications heretofore submitted to the FHA or
VA or a licensed Property Appraiser and to obtain an FHA or VA Compliance Inspection Report or an Appraiser's Completion Inspection Report showing
satisfactory compliance on or before _____ days after buyer loan approval. If dwelling is not completed within thirty (30) days from the date
specified, Buyer shall be entitled to refund of the earnest money paid herewith and in said event, this contract shall be terminated. Buyer's sole remedy for
failure of Seller to construct the dwelling and complete the same as herein specified shall be limited to a return of the earnest money deposit. Receipt by
Seller of FHA or VA Final Compliance Inspection Report or Appraiser Completion Inspection Report shall constitute evidence of completion.

7. FAILURE TO CLOSE LOAN: In the event Buyer shall be approved for said loan and shall fail or refuse to close this transaction by executing the mortgage
documents and pay the balance due within 5 days after tender of closing, the earnest money deposit paid herein shall be retained by Seller as liquidated
damages and this contract shall be terminated upon expiration of said 5 day period.

8. SELLER'S COVENANTS: Seller shall at closing deliver a good and sufficient warranty deed to Buyer conveying a marketable title free and clear of all
encumbrances and exceptions other than the usual and ordinary exceptions as to future taxes, covenants, restrictions, and utility agreements.

9. CONSTRUCTION FINANCING will be at the expense of the seller.

10. The buyer of a one- or two-family residential dwelling unit has the right to have all deposit funds (up to 10 percent of the purchase price) deposited in
an interest-bearing escrow account. This right may be waived, in writing by the Buyer. Escrow deposit (up to 10 percent of the purchase price) is
_____ required _____ waived.

11. ADDITIONAL TERMS AND CONDITIONS IF ANY: Buyer understands that a homeowners association is in place in (name of community) and that annual
and special assessments as determined by Board of Directors of the association will be levied against the property and unpaid assessments can become liens
against the property. Buyer further understands that the $ _____ annual assessment for _____ is not an indication of the level
of future assessments.

12. This contract constitutes the sole and entire agreement between the parties and no modification, written or verbal shall be binding upon either party
unless in writing signed by both parties and attached hereto. This contract shall inure to the benefit of the heirs, personal representatives and successors
and assigns of the Seller and Buyer respectively.

IN WITNESS WHEREOF the parties have hereto set their hands and seals this date/s shown below:

WITNESS (As to Buyer)

_____   _____

     Buyer   DATE

WITNESS (As to Seller)

_____   _____

     Buyer   DATE

_____   BY _____

                      DATE

Figure 3-14. Purchaser Information Form

Purchaser's Name _____ Age _____

Spouse _____ Age _____

Present Address _____

Property Address _____

Present Phone Number _____ New Phone Number _____

Broker _____ Phone _____

_____

Employment Information:

Husband's Employer _____

Length of Employment _____ Transferred _____

Approximate Annual Income _____

Business Phone _____

Wife's Employer _____

Length of Employment _____ Transferred _____

Approximate Annual Income _____

Business Phone _____

Personal Information:

Number of Children _____ Ages _____

Names _____

Hobbies (Husband) _____

Hobbies (Wife) _____

Special Interests (Family) _____

_____

_____

Figure 3-15. Contract Processing Checklist

Salesperson: _____ Community: _____

Buyer: _____ Date: _____

Address of Property: _____

	Date	Initial
1. Check received	____	____
Additional Amount Due: _____		
Date Due: _____ Received _____		
2. Contract typed and signed	____	____
a. Buydown Addendum	____	____
b. Contingency Addendum	____	____
c. Option Addendum and Additional Work Authorization	____	____
d. FHA Addendum	____	____
e. Estimated Monthly Payment	____	____
f. Price Breakdown	____	____
g. Purchaser Information Sheet	____	____
h. Color Selection Sheet	____	____
i. Commission Schedule	____	____
3. Mortgage appointment—Date:	____	
Time:	____	
Lender:	____	
4. Deed Restrictions and HOA Documents (if applicable)	____	____
5. Warranty Book and Sample Limited Warranty	____	____

6. Special Instructions _____

_____

_____

Secretary _____   Check(s) to account

Executed Copy to: Lender _____

Buyer _____

Copy to: Title Co. _____

Broker _____

Color Keyed on Plat   _____

Figure 3-16. Sample Purchaser Letter

Date

Mr. and Mrs. Jack Brown
100 Smith Road
Anywhere, USA

Dear Mr. and Mrs. Brown:

Thank you for buying a _____
home! Enclosed please find a copy of your executed purchase agreement and other
documents relating to your purchase.

Once your home is completed, and before you take possession, you will meet with your
salesperson for a "Home Introduction." It is necessary that you allow at least twenty-four
hours between your "Home Introduction" and your actual closing time. The purpose of the
"Home Introduction" is to orient you with the specific features and operation of your new
home. The salesperson will present a detailed list of items in your home and call your
attention to each item. Please inspect these items carefully to make sure that these items
meet with your approval as being complete and in working order. After you are satisfied
with your home, you will be asked to sign an Affidavit of Acceptable Completion, stating
that you are happy with the condition of your new home and that all items are in good
working order. Your signing of this affidavit assures our management of the company that
your home is complete and you are satisfied with it.

Our reputation is built on honesty and fairness with our customers, letting them know what
to expect. Recognizing this, we have developed an easy-to-read manual that outlines our
Warranty Service procedure. Your salesperson will present this to you and review various
problems that may occur and our responsibility with respect to these items. Your
salesperson will outline some of the common occurrences and answer any questions you
may have.

It is our desire to serve you in such a way that you are pleased with our product and our
service. We wish you many years of happiness in your new _____
  home. If you have any additional questions, please feel free to contact your salesperson.

Sincerely,

_____
Sales Director

Enclosure

Figure 3-17. Sample New Home Price Breakdown Form

Purchaser's Name _____ Address _____

Projected Closing Date _____ Lot _____ Block _____

Base Price $ _____

Premium Lot Charge $ _____

Elevation Charge $ _____

Options:

Carpet Upgrade _____ $ _____

Fireplace $ _____

Intercom $ _____

Screened Enclosed Patio $ _____
    Size _____ × _____

Additional Concrete (diagram attached) $ _____
    Size _____ × _____

Refrigerator $ _____
    Model No. _____

Upgrade Range $ _____
    Model No. _____

Extra Outlets (Not on ground fault breaker) $ _____
(diagram attached)

Ceramic Tile: Foyer # _____ $ _____

Attic Ladder $ _____

TOTAL OPTIONS $ _____

TOTAL SALES PRICE $ _____

_____   _____
Office Approval   Salesperson

_____   _____
Date   Purchaser

                                             _____
                                             Purchaser

- Change order: all exceptional changes must be submitted on a work authorization/modifications form (Figure 3-18). Commitments and prices for non-standard options are at the sole discretion of the builder and should not be encouraged in most circumstances. The processing time and extra costs involved in production and administration usually do not warrant making these adjustments in standardized home products. If changes are critical to a sale, the salesperson should be prepared to justify exceptional changes to the builder.
- Customer selection sheet: standard color and material selections are entered on a selection sheet (Figure 3-19) and submitted prior to the start of construction. The salesperson should monitor and check purchaser selections carefully to prevent incompatible color combinations between adjacent properties that would decrease the value of the environment. Normally, these situations can be handled through suggestion rather than restriction. The purchaser should sign the selection sheet, which should then be submitted to the sales director for processing. A copy of all documents should be placed in the pending sale file.
- Homeowners association documents: in any community with a homeowners association, each purchaser should be given a package of documents and asked to sign a receipt (Figure 3-20) for all the listed documents. Figure 3-21 illustrates a sample agreement to join a homeowners association.
- Purchaser financial analysis: salespersons should use this form (Figure 3-22) to present projected costs to potential purchasers. It is important that salespersons calculate accurately and be knowledgeable about interest rates, closing costs, and mortgage types.
- Contact log: Figure 3-23 illustrates a contact log that should be stapled to the front of each pending sale file to record any substantive issues, assurances, or requests that come up during telephone or on-site discussions.

The salesperson is responsible for assembling documents and information required to process a sale and for following the progress of the transaction until it has been consummated. This includes collection of additional deposits due. In the event the central office is not in receipt of an additional deposit on the due date, a letter of cancellation should be issued.

Goal #4: Courtesy and Quality. Delivery of a quality home according to an appropriate schedule, and responsive customer service for corrections or adjustments needed after occupancy, are the final, crucial goals of successful new home sales. An important policy to include in any manual is that consumers be treated courteously and respectfully at all times during the sales process. Salespersons, secretaries, management, and every member of the builder's team must attempt to resolve questions or disagreements properly and in a spirit

Figure 3-18. Sample Modifications Form

Purchaser _____

Lot _____ Block _____ Floor Plan _____

I request prices for the following modifications:

_____   _____
Date   Purchaser

                              _____
                              Purchaser

	Price	Initials Builder	Initials Purchaser

I agree to make the modifications for the prices listed above. For the changes that I am unable to make, I have so indicated by writing NO in place of the price.

_____   _____
Date   (Name of Community)

I agree to pay the prices listed above for the requested modifications. These costs should: [   ] be included in my mortgage [   ] be paid in cash: 50% upon execution of this form and 50% at closing.

_____   _____
Date   Purchaser

Figure 3-19. Sample Selection Sheet

Customer _____   Community _____
New Address _____   Exterior Plan # _____
Model Number _____   Date _____

Kitchen:

Appliance Color _____   Counter Top _____
Cabinets _____   Flooring _____

Master Bath:

Fixtures _____   Tile _____
Vanity _____   Flooring _____

Guest Bath:

Fixtures _____   Tile _____
Vanity _____   Flooring _____

Half Bath:

Fixtures _____   Flooring _____
Vanity _____

Carpeting _____   Foyer Flooring _____
Lighting Fixtures _____

Please consider your selections very carefully. There will be absolutely no changes permitted after the selection sheet has been submitted.

_____
Purchaser

By: _____
    Salesperson

_____
Purchaser

of cooperation. All staff should remember that small problems become large through inattention and that a "no" is better received when it is delivered early with a full explanation of why a "yes" cannot be given. Problems that cannot be resolved directly by a salesperson should be referred to the sales director or the builder immediately.

Finally, nothing sells a home better than the assurance of quality and the peace of mind that comes from the builder's guarantee of service after the sale. All salespersons should emphasize the builder's history, credibility, and reputation in the community as a quality builder.

Figure 3-20. Sample Receipt for Homeowners Association Documents

(COMMUNITY) HOMEOWNERS ASSOCIATION, INC.

_____

_____

_____

As owner of _____ , I acknowledge
receipt of the following documents:

- Articles of Incorporation of (Community) Homeowners Association, Inc.
- By-Laws of (Community) Homeowners Association, Inc.
- Declaration of Covenants, Conditions, and Restrictions of (Community) Homeowners Association, Inc.
- Declaration of Restrictions, (Deed Restrictions) for (Community), Section _____.

I (we) have read the foregoing and have received the documents listed above.

_____   _____
Date   Buyer

                                     _____
                                     Buyer

Figure 3-21. Sample Agreement to Join Homeowners Association

AGREEMENT TO JOIN

(COMMUNITY) MASTER COMMUNITY ASSOCIATION

RE: _____

_____

_____

Buyer hereby acknowledges that (Company), the Developer (Community), intends to establish a Master Community Association which would encompass most of the (Community) Development. The Master Association would provide for the maintenance of the common areas, recreational areas and all other common facilities within the Development.

If a Master Community Association is established encompassing _____ and other parts of the (Community), whether in whole or in part, every owner of a lot or dwelling unit in shall be a member thereof and shall be subject to an assessment for maintenance and operation thereof, and all the terms, conditions and provisions of the Declaration of Covenants, Articles of Incorporation and By-Laws of such Master Community Association.

I (We) have read the foregoing and agree to join in the above described Declaration of Covenants if requested by (Company) and encumber the above described property. (Company) hereby represents that in no event shall Buyer's assessment exceed (amount) per year for the first (number of years) years from the date of closing of the above described property by Buyer.

_____

Buyer

_____

Buyer

(COMPANY)

By: _____

Dated: _____

Figure 3-22. Purchaser Financial Analysis

Presentation to _____

Address _____

City _____ State _____ Zip _____ Tel _____

	% Financing	% Financing
Deposit upon signing Purchase Agreement	$ _____	$ _____
Mortgage amount	_____	_____
Balance, cash at closing	_____	_____
TOTAL PURCHASE PRICE	$ _____	$ _____
Buyers total closing costs	$ _____	$ _____
Monthly mortgage—principal and interest	_____	_____
Real estate taxes, per month	_____	_____
Homeowner's insurance, per month	_____	_____
TOTAL ESTIMATED MONTHLY PAYMENT	$ _____	$ _____

ALL FIGURES ARE PRESENTED ON AN ESTIMATED BASIS ONLY AND ARE SUBJECT TO VERIFICATION, CHANGE OR REVISION. THIS PRESENTATION IS NOT AN OFFER TO SELL NOR AN OFFER TO BUY.

Estimated Pre-Paid Escrow Items
(Collected from Buyer at Closing)

MGIC Ins., 1-yr	$ _____	Date _____ 19 _____
Insurance, 14-mo	_____	
R E Taxes, 2-mo	_____	_____
1st Month Payment	_____	Sales Associate
TOTAL	$ _____	_____
		Business Associate

47

Figure 3-23. Purchaser Contact Log

Purchaser's Name _____

Telephone _____

Property Address _____

Mailing Address _____

City, State, Zip _____

Date	Summary of Remarks

Chapter Four

Hiring and Preparing the Sales Team

A builder's sales staff is the "front line" in a successful home sales operation, and sales positions are among the most important in any building company. The builder who chooses to develop an in-house sales staff must consider each new hiring effort an opportunity to strengthen the sales team and improve sales performance. The likelihood of hiring the right person improves through the use of a systematic hiring process. To this end, the steps recommended in this chapter should make the hiring process easier and more successful.

Defining the Position

The first step in hiring is to define clearly the position to be filled and the compensation to be provided. This definition process minimizes the chances of hiring the right person for the wrong position or vice versa.

When defining sales positions, the builder should consider the following three major sales responsibilities:

- Sales director: sales management and administration of sales staff and facilities (often in addition to selling responsibilities).
- Salesperson: selling new homes, whether on scattered sites or in a single community.
- Support staff: secretarial and receptionist services, provided as traffic volume warrants.

If one is not available, a job description should be written for each position. Existing job descriptions should be updated to ensure they reflect any evolution of the position during a previous employee's tenure. Similarly, the compensation program should be defined in writing and updated as necessary.

Figures 4-1 and 4-2 provide sample job descriptions for salesperson and sales director. They should be adjusted as needed to reflect the authority, responsibilities, communication levels, and daily functions of a builder's organization.

Creating the Applicant Pool

This step involves developing a pool of applicants from whom to choose. Most applicants learn about jobs through word of mouth or classified advertising. It is advisable to pursue both avenues. Sample recruitment ads are provided in Figure 4-3.

Typical methods for word-of-mouth advertising include the following:

- Calling friends and colleagues for recommendations. This activity has the occasional benefit of revealing interest in a position from the very person called.
- Asking for recommendations from current employees in similar positions.
- Attending industry association meetings to discuss the position informally.

Some of the best candidates come through word of mouth. Their abilities and probable success are relatively easy to judge since the candidates are known to the builder and/or others in the organization.

Evaluating Candidate Resumes

All applicants should be asked to submit resumes without any advance commitment for an interview. Interviewing is a time-consuming process, and that time should be reserved exclusively for serious candidates. An applicant unwilling or unable to provide a resume is behaving unprofessionally and should not be considered seriously. Conversely, some candidates will attempt to obtain immediate interviews when personally delivering their resumes. While their aggressiveness and strong motivation are commendable, the interview should not be granted at that time. Instead, the builder should proceed with resume evaluations. This process should result in a list of serious candidates to be interviewed, ideally not fewer than three or more than seven.

A resume reveals far more than the objective information it outlines. Careful resume screening saves interviewing time by pre-selecting candidates most likely to succeed in the job. Figure 4-4 provides a resume evaluation/rating form that will aid in making subjective and objective judgments on each candidate prior to an interview. The numbers 3, 2 and 0 on this form are intended to represent good, fair, or

Figure 4-1. Job Description: Salesperson

I. Authority

Under the supervision of the sales director, and in conformity with the laws of the state: prepares and executes contracts for the purchase of new homes; quotes prices and offering terms as specified in writing by sales directors; receives offers to purchase from customers (in writing and with specified deposit) and transmits to sales director; accepts deposit and other purchase related monies and transmits to the sales director or accounting department; assists in arranging purchase mortgage financing; executes and transmits color and material selections, change orders, and related construction documents.

II. Responsibility

Responsible for meeting personal sales goals and objectives.

Responsible for representing the company and its products fully and accurately to the public.

Responsible for service and follow-up to prospects and purchasers from the time of their initial introduction to the company's homes and community.

Responsible for maintaining clear and accurate marketing and sales information according to the company's reporting system.

Responsible for completeness and accuracy of all purchase file documents.

Responsible for the general condition of model and sales office interiors, and for reporting deficiencies to the sales director.

Responsible for full knowledge of the assigned community, company homes for sale, pricing, pre-arranged financing, standard construction practices, and company policies and procedures.

III. Communication and Reporting

Communicates directly with other salespersons in the assigned community and other company communities.

Communicates directly with lenders, title companies, and others involved in the purchase transaction.

Communicates directly with potential consumers and buyers.

Communicates directly and through the sales director with other departments and divisions of the company.

Reports directly to the sales director.

IV. Duties

Performs tasks assigned by the sales director including, but not limited to, competitive product shopping, product knowledge exercises, sales technique reviews.

Maintains prospect files and marketing reports.

Staffs the information center and models according to schedules assigned by the sales director.

Conducts personal tours of model homes and information center for all prospects visiting the community according to a rotational schedule defined by the sales director.

Makes planned sales presentations including, but not limited to, greeting, qualifying, demonstrating, siting, and closing.

Assists brokers and their clients in the purchase of company products.

Maintains and organizes sales collateral materials in an adequate supply for daily use.

Performs follow-up and self-prospecting activities to maximize sales.

Maintains good customer relations by prompt and courteous attention to the needs of prospects and purchasers.

Participates in professional training and seeks opportunities to learn and develop professional skills.

Signed: Salesperson _____ Date _____

Supervisor _____ Date _____

Figure 4-2. Job Description: Sales Director

I.   **Authority**

Under the supervision of the vice president and officers of the company: hires, directs, trains, and fires salespersons and support staff within the assigned community(ies); reviews and approves all contracts and purchase-related documents in conformity with local, state, and federal laws; receives deposits and other purchase-related monies for deposit in escrow accounts or delivery to the accounting department; makes binding arbitration decisions in the case of commission or other disputes among salespersons.

II. **Responsibility**

Responsible for representing the company and its products fully and accurately to the public.

Responsible for meeting the overall sales and profitability objectives of the company.

Responsible for daily salesperson and support staff work schedules, productivity, special assignments, and training.

Responsible for monitoring and evaluation procedures and reports.

Responsible for the overall condition of the sales environment including models, information center, and sales/administrative supplies.

Responsible for the completeness and accuracy of all files on available homes and purchases in process.

III. **Communication and Reporting**

Communicates directly with company employees and principals at all levels.

Communicates directly with bank executives, title officers, and others involved in transaction process.

Reports directly to the vice president or officers of the company.

IV. **Duties**

Performs all tasks assigned by the vice president or other specifically supervising officer(s) of the company including, but not limited to, management of the sales and support staff in designated communities.

Reviews and monitors the productivity and progress of salespersons and their transactions.

Assists salespersons appropriately in the sales process, customer service, follow-up, and self-prospecting activities.

Conducts regular sales meetings for the purpose of training, transmitting information from other departments/divisions of the company, identifying and resolving problems, and motivating salespersons to top performance.

Compiles periodic monitoring and evaluation reports, competitive product and market research data, and customer or staff suggestions for transmittal to marketing staff.

Participates in all weekly meetings of the sales team as well as periodically attending appropriate general management meetings.

Facilitates the flow of information and documents between the sales team and other departments or divisions of the company.

Monitors the progress and availability of products in the assigned community(ies).

Manages and facilitates the broker cooperation program.

Arbitrates commission or other disputes among salespersons.

Maintains good customer relations through prompt and courteous attention to the needs of prospects and purchasers.

Follows through all contracts to closing.

Signed: Sales Director _____ Date _____

          Supervisor _____ Date _____

Figure 4-3. Sample Recruitment Ads

SITE SALES DIRECTOR

Exciting new community of ___(type of housing)___ needs a dynamic proven professional to build our team. Challenging, but supportive atmosphere. Rigorous, but pleasant selection process. Fantastic monetary and career rewards to winner. Send resume and income history in complete confidence to ___(address or newspaper box)___.

SITE SALES ASSOCIATE

Exciting new community of ___(type of housing)___ needs a dynamic proven professional to join our team. Stimulating and congenial atmosphere. Rigorous, but pleasant selection process. Fantastic rewards to winner. Send resume and income history in complete confidence to ___(address or newspaper box)___. Do it today!

REAL ESTATE SECRETARY/RECEPTIONIST

Exciting new community of ___(type of housing)___ needs a very special person to fill the most important and challenging position on our team. Congenial and supportive atmosphere. Rigorous, but pleasant selection process. Significant rewards to winner. Send resume and salary history in complete confidence to ___(address or newspaper box)___. Do it today!

poor. The fourth column contains a multiplier factor that weighs each item for relative importance in the evaluation. The assigned rating is multiplied by the multiplier, and the result entered in column five. Addition of all the numbers in column five provides a numerical score for this resume to compare with other resumes received. Since different reviewers may define good, fair, and poor differently, it is best to have one person perform all ratings. In addition, noting a minimum of three questions relating to each "interview resume" can improve interviewing efficiency.

Interviewing

Interviewing should be viewed as a planned, continuing process, not a one-time event. The process normally consists of the following stages:

- The interview, be it a single meeting or as many as three separate interviews on two or more days.
- Information-gathering/recommendation from previous employers.
- Written self-evaluation.
- Meetings for interviewers (if there is more than one) to discuss relevant qualifications of leading contenders.

Interviews

First interviews are normally conducted by the company representative to whom the new employee will report, usually either the builder or sales director (if already on staff). This individual will either choose the appropriate candidate (as in the case when the builder is the sole interviewer) or narrow the candidate list to two or three for further interviewing.

If a second round of interviews is planned, additional company decision-makers interview top candidates. The original interviewer should talk briefly with each candidate first, then pass the applicant to second or third company representatives. Each of these interviews should be

---

Figure 4-4. Resume Evaluation/Rating Form

1. **First Impression**
   1. Resume complete, concise, current, well-written ..... 3 2 0 1 __
   2. Resume neatly formatted and presented ..... 3 2 0 1 __

2. **Education**
   3. Level appropriate for prospects and colleagues ..... 3 2 0 1 __
   4. Adequate continuing education ..... 3 2 0 1 __
   5. Ability to complete a course of study ..... 3 2 0 1 __
   6. Is state-licensed agent/broker ..... 3 2 0 1 __

3. **Community Involvement/Hobbies**
   7. Appropriate level of involvement ..... 3 2 0 1 __
   8. Includes "social" involvements ..... 3 2 0 1 __

4. **Honors and Achievements**
   9. Competes successfully for recognition ..... 3 2 0 2 __

5. **Salary History**
   10. Salary within appropriate range for your compensation ..... 3 2 0 2 __

6. **Job History**
   11. Experience directly related or indirectly appropriate for new home sales ..... 3 2 0 3 __
   12. Has held one job in last ten years for three or more years ..... 3 2 0 3 __
   13. Has been internally promoted ..... 3 2 0 2 __
   14. Has made "positive" career moves ..... 3 2 0 2 __
   15. Demonstrates a success pattern ..... 3 2 0 3 __

Total Score __

If the decision is made to interview the candidate, note three or more questions to ask that relate to the resume.

conducted with only one company representative and only one candidate present.

Interview Questions

Figure 4-5 offers a list of possible interview questions. Certain questions are identified for sales director interviews and are less appropriate for salespersons. Questions for salespersons, however, can also be asked of sales director candidates. Questions should be carefully chosen from this list to ensure the interviewer spends far more time listening to the candidate than talking. Immediately after every interview, the interviewer should note initial reactions, candidate strengths and weaknesses, and a general opinion of the candidate's suitability for the position. In addition, an interview evaluation/rating form (Figure 4-6) should be completed for each candidate to facilitate cross comparison.

Previous Employer Recommendations

No candidate should reach the final interview stage until personal contact has been made with—and a positive recommendation received from—the candidate's previous employer(s). This process is often completed before any interviews are scheduled but must be completed prior to second interviews. The most important question to ask a former employer is "Would you employ this individual again?"

Self-Evaluations

At the conclusion of the first personal interview, many builders ask candidates to complete written self-evaluations. This self-evaluation can be used in the second interview as the basis for new questions, can be compared with an earlier evaluation of the candidate to gauge self-esteem, and provides a cursory indication of written communications skills. A sample self-evaluation form is provided in Figure 4-7.

Hiring

The offer to hire is frequently made by telephone but should be confirmed by letter. This letter should reiterate the position title, place of work, starting date, and time and place the new employee will be welcomed on his or her first day. The tone of the letter should be congratulatory and upbeat.

Company Orientation

A salesperson or sales director lacking adequate knowledge of a builder's organization and products cannot be expected to function effi-

Figure 4-5. Sample Interview Questions

Salesperson and Sales Directors

I.   **Background/Experience:**

Specific questions should be taken from resume evaluation/rating form (Figure 4-4).

Why are you thinking of taking a new position at this time?

What are your reasons for leaving your last job?

What recent accomplishment are you most proud of?

II. **Goals/Objectives:**

What would you most like to accomplish or learn next?

Do you set goals for yourself? Long or short-term goals? What are these goals now?

What is your greatest asset and liability? What have you done recently to deal with this weakness?

III. **Specific Knowledge:**

What is a "planned" presentation? Can you list the five major components of a new home sales presentation?

What is your most successful closing technique? Can you name or describe some other techniques you have used? What is the "silent close"?

How many times, would you estimate, does a salesperson have to close before an average sale is made?

Can you name or describe several ways to overcome objections?

What do you think are the biggest mistakes many salespersons make?

What are the traits of a professional salesperson and a successful closer?

Should a salesperson relate better to the product, or the buyer?

How would you describe the role of construction staff in the sales process?

What is a "mystery shop"?

What is customer service? When does it begin and end?

Can you describe the difference between "selling," "showing," and "merchandising" a model home?

How do you feel model homes should be shown?

What is "feature/benefit" demonstration?

IV. **Attitudes and Working Habits:**

What does "professional dress" mean to you?

Do you do anything special when you answer the telephone or greet an arrival at the information center?

What part of the sales job do you find most or least enjoyable?

Do you work to live, or live to work?

What sort of hours have you been keeping in your most recent job?

What have you done to improve yourself and your professional skills in the past year?

Why are you in a sales position?

V.   **Specific Knowledge Questions for Sales Directors:**

How do you define the difference between sales management and marketing management?

What role does research play in the responsibilities of a sales director?

Rank these sources of leads in terms of generating traffic and generating sales: Newspaper ads, magazine ads, signage, customer referrals, direct mail.

What players would you involve in sales meetings, and what would be on a typical agenda?

What percentage of your meetings would you allocate to: administration, education, motivation?

What are the most important mistakes unsuccessful sales directors make?

What is the difference between responsibility and authority?

Does authority have to be earned?

What sales training techniques have been most effective for you?

How would you establish and sustain a broker cooperation program for sales?

As a sales director, who and what should you control?

What type of reports do you need to manage sales and salespersons?

What steps would you take to manage sales in this or any other new company?

If you were hiring a new salesperson, what steps would you take, and what qualities would you look for?

What would your new salesperson training process consist of, in general terms? When would it begin and end?

What responsibilities would you want or expect with this or any other new company?

VI. **Attitude and Management Philosophy Questions for Sales Directors:**

Do you feel you should have the responsibility to hire and fire salespersons?

Are you people-oriented? Why is this important in a sales director?

What is the best personality for a sales director, and why: autocratic, benevolent, democratic?

How importantly does motivation rank in terms of sales characteristics and why?

Should a sales director's compensation program include incentives tied to the product or the sales staff, and why?

What authority would you want as sales director, and why? Is authority earned? If so, how?

What do salespersons like most and least about sales directors?

How do you build consensus and avoid confrontation?

Figure 4-6. Interview Evaluation/Rating Form

Candidate: _____ Telephone: (_____)_____

Position/Community: _____ Date: _____

Other Sales Experience: _____ yes _____ no _____ years

Real Estate Sales _____ yes _____ no _____ years
Experience:

Sales Director Experience: _____ yes _____ no _____ years

Type of Product: _____

Smoker: _____ Other Habits: _____

Did the candidate "ask" for the job: _____

	Exc.	Good	Fair	Poor	Total	Comments
Greeting Impression	3	2	1	0	_____	_____
Overall Appearance/Grooming	3	2	1	0	_____	_____
Composure/Poise	3	2	1	0	_____	_____
Communication Skills/Grammar	3	2	1	0	_____	_____
Eye Contact/Empathy	3	2	1	0	_____	_____
Assertiveness/Ego	3	2	1	0	_____	_____
Personality/Enthusiasm	3	2	1	0	_____	_____
Appropriate or Direct Experience	3	2	1	0	_____	_____
Pattern of Success	3	2	1	0	_____	_____
Breadth of Experience	3	2	1	0	_____	_____
Goal Setter	3	2	1	0	_____	_____
Reason for Interviewing	3	2	1	0	_____	_____
Reason for Leaving Last Job	3	2	1	0	_____	_____
Sales Skills (general)	3	2	1	0	_____	_____
Planned Presentation Experience	3	2	1	0	_____	_____
Closing Skills	3	2	1	0	_____	_____
Self Starter	3	2	1	0	_____	_____
Team Player	3	2	1	0	_____	_____
Dedicated Worker	3	2	1	0	_____	_____
Can Control Details	3	2	1	0	_____	_____
Interpersonal Skills	3	2	1	0	_____	_____
Management Skills	10	8	3	0	_____	_____
Management Philosophy	10	8	3	0	_____	_____
			Total		_____	

General Comments: _____
_____

ciently. Yet many builders provide no formal orientation. Instead, new sales employees learn on-the-job either through trial-and-error or trial by fire. This informal orientation process is inefficient and often has a negative impact on sales performance. While smart builders hire only skilled, experienced salespersons, formal orientation and continuing training are effective methods for ensuring sales effort continuity and top performance by new employees of all skill levels. The orientation program described in this chapter details those topics essential to effective sales performance.

Figure 4-7. Candidate Self-Evaluation

On a scale of 1 to 10, with 10 the highest score, rate yourself on each of the following:

_____ ability to close

_____ ability to qualify

_____ ability to empathize

_____ ability to motivate

_____ ability to control

_____ ability to lead

_____ ability to educate

_____ ability to organize

_____ ability to compete

_____ ability to think positively

_____ ability to create a positive sales environment

_____ ability to overcome objections

_____ ability to demonstrate

_____ ability to prospect

_____ ability to provide customer service

_____ ability to plan

_____ ability to administer

_____ ability to communicate

_____ ability to establish goals

_____ ability to achieve goals

_____ ability to follow through

_____ ability to speak

_____ ability to listen

Summarize your strengths and weaknesses:

What are your long- and short-term goals?

The company orientation is particulary important for new sales employees because they will use information about the company, its history, and the builder during the sales process to establish credibility. Any written materials that can be referenced at a later time—a company brochure or written company description and history—should be given to the new sales employee during the orientation.

Orientation Responsibility

The sales director or builder should conduct new salesperson orientations. New sales director orientation usually falls upon the director's immediate supervisor—often the builder. Orientation for onsite brokers and associates is usually coordinated by the key staff person with overall responsibility for marketing and sales—again, usually the builder.

Orientation: Five Steps

The company orientation usually consists of five steps:

- Performing the company tour and introducing new employees to central office staff, key employees in other divisions, chief executive, and all members of the marketing and sales staff.
- Reviewing company history and organization, including review of current projects; discussion of goals, organization, and subsidiary companies; and briefing on company management.
- Obtaining information for the personnel file, registering for payroll and benefit programs, completing forms for income tax withholding, and providing information on company policies and procedures.
- Conducting the sales environment orientation. At the information center, the new employee should receive instructions on office procedures and be issued office keys, a desk, supplies, and the sales polices and procedures manual.
- Introducing the marketing and sales system.

Figure 4-8 summarizes a two-week orientation plan for new sales staff on a simple bar chart. Rigorous adherence to each of the steps in this orientation plan will ensure the success of each new salesperson.

Introduction

The first step in orientation is traditionally an introduction to the company, its headquarters, and central office staff. New sales employees should be introduced to construction and operations staff and/or principals and assisted with employment paperwork. At this time, new employees should sign an employment agreement (Figure 4-9), job description, and compensation agreement (Figure 4-10) and be given copies for personal files.

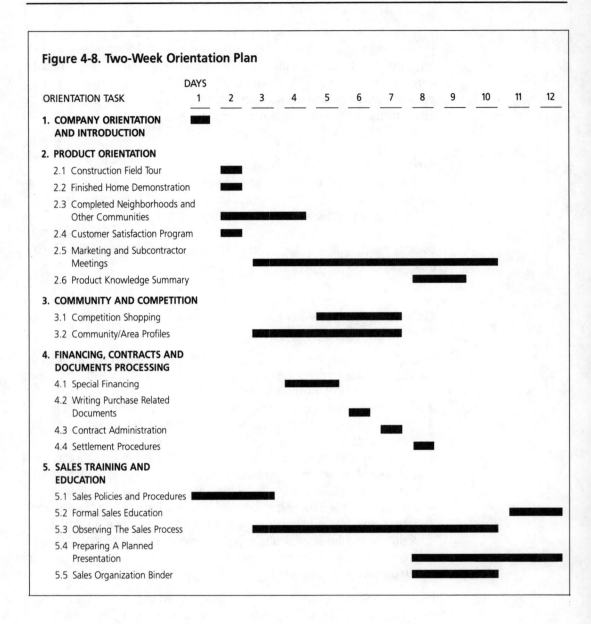

Figure 4-8. Two-Week Orientation Plan

ORIENTATION TASK	DAYS
1. COMPANY ORIENTATION AND INTRODUCTION	Day 1
2. PRODUCT ORIENTATION	
2.1 Construction Field Tour	Day 2
2.2 Finished Home Demonstration	Day 2
2.3 Completed Neighborhoods and Other Communities	Days 2–4
2.4 Customer Satisfaction Program	Day 2
2.5 Marketing and Subcontractor Meetings	Days 3–10
2.6 Product Knowledge Summary	Days 8–9
3. COMMUNITY AND COMPETITION	
3.1 Competition Shopping	Days 5–7
3.2 Community/Area Profiles	Days 3–7
4. FINANCING, CONTRACTS AND DOCUMENTS PROCESSING	
4.1 Special Financing	Days 4–5
4.2 Writing Purchase Related Documents	Day 6
4.3 Contract Administration	Day 7
4.4 Settlement Procedures	Day 8
5. SALES TRAINING AND EDUCATION	
5.1 Sales Policies and Procedures	Days 1–3
5.2 Formal Sales Education	Days 11–12
5.3 Observing The Sales Process	Days 3–10
5.4 Preparing A Planned Presentation	Days 8–12
5.5 Sales Organization Binder	Days 8–10

Product Orientation

Product knowledge is the basis of all sales. Every new salesperson, sales director, and broker associate should be made thoroughly familiar with the company's products very early in the training and orientation process. Several days are usually devoted to product knowledge exercises. Product training sets the stage for sales training, during which the employee learns how to build the perceived value of the new homes through a feature-benefit presentation.

Product knowledge training is often divided into the following four segments:

- Construction field tour conducted by the builder or superintendent, including a tour of homes in various stages of construction to illustrate construction phasing, quality standards, and standard construction practices. Procedures for clear, complete communication between sales and construction personnel should be discussed at this time.
- Finished home demonstration to demonstrate standard construction features; highlight the quality of finished work, materials, and products; and illustrate the care taken during construction to ensure consistent high quality in the finished product.
- Tour of completed neighborhoods and other new communities to see the builder's completed products, enabling the new salesperson to speak confidently to consumers about the lasting value of the builder's homes and communities.
- Introduction to the purchaser satisfaction program and meeting with marketing and subcontracting firms to provide in-depth information about the models, merchandising tools, major mechanical systems, and special features in the product offerings. Useful techniques for treating new home features and compelling marketing words for referring to products and materials within the home are often discovered in such meetings. At the conclusion of orientation, sales employees should test themselves on their newly accrued knowledge. Any suggestions, corrections, or recommendations should be discussed with the sales director and/or builder for possible implementation.

Figure 4-9. Sample Letter of Agreement

By this letter and attachments, ___(company name)___ and ___(employee name)___ agree to employment as ___(position title)___ beginning ___(date)___ .

Employee hereby agrees to the terms and conditions outlined in the Job Description, Commission Agreement, and Sales Policies and Procedures and acknowledges receipt of same.

Employee further agrees, at all times, to abide by local, state, and federal regulations governing real estate transactions. Failure to do so is cause for immediate termination.

In the event of termination of this agreement, notice shall be given by either party to the other 30 days before such termination shall become effective, except that termination for cause shall be immediately effective.

In the event of termination, all documents, records, files, and information related to ___(company name)___ shall remain the sole property of ___(company name)___ .

Attachments: Signed Job Description
              Signed Commission Agreement

Figure 4-10. Sample Compensation Agreement

By the signature below, ___(employee)___ understands that the commissions currently paid by ___(company)___ at ___(community)___ are as follows:

1. On the first $1,000,000 in sales during the calendar year, a commission of 1 percent of the base selling price exclusive of options and extras.

2. On the volume between $1,000,001 and $2,000,000 in sales during the same calendar year, a commission of 1½ percent of the base selling price exclusive of options and extras.

3. On the volume between $2,000,001 and $3,000,000 in sales during the same calendar year, a commission of 1¾ percent of the selling price inclusive of options and extras.

4. On the volume in excess of $3,000,000 in sales during the same calendar year, a commission of 2 percent of the selling price inclusive of options and extras.

Said commissions will also be paid in the case of all cooperative sales that involve real estate brokers and broker associates.

Said commissions will also be paid on homes sold to employees participating in the Home Purchase Employee Bonus Plan. Commission will be paid on employee home purchases not qualifying under the above bonus plan.

Employee understands that commissions may be changed, from time to time, at the sole discretion of ___(company)___, in which case employee will be notified of the changes in writing and be asked to approve a new Commission Agreement. Failure to do so will result in termination of employment upon 30-day notice.

In the event of termination for any cause, employee will receive ½ of all commissions due from pending sales. A Pending Sale is defined as a completed and fully signed purchase contract as well as a loan application completed and returned to the lender unless the purchase is all cash. Employee understands that commission retainage is necessary to assure optimum service to the consumer by other individuals subsequent to the termination.

_____
Employee Signature

_____
Date

Community and Competition

The average new home consumer visits six to ten new home communities before making a purchase decision. Therefore, the salesperson must know the competition in order sell effectively against it. Knowledge of the competition will enable the salesperson to build comparative value around the strengths and weaknesses of competing products.

Shopping the Competition. A new salesperson should examine between two to four competitive developments located within the market area, allowing one or two hours per community over a period of several days. While salespersons should feel free to identify themselves, they may wish to shop as consumers from time to time to see and hear exactly what the consumer is experiencing. The competition evaluation form (Figure 3-5) should be used to accumulate data on these other communities.

Community Knowledge. With respect to the community in which the new salesperson will be working, he or she should not only know the community and its amenities but experience them from a fresh perspective. For example, salespersons should learn not only the name of the public elementary school but the name of the principal as well. Salespersons might shop at the pro shop and visit the club house at the local golf course. Experiences such as these will provide in-depth area knowledge useful in personalizing sales presentations.

Financing, Contracts, and Document Processing

Salespersons should be knowledgeable in the use and processing of all sales-related documents. Since each builder's documents differ in some respects from all others, specific training for new employees may be required. This training is usually divided into the following four subject areas:

Special Financing Options. Training in special financing options should include both the technical aspects of financing and techniques for explaining the program to consumers clearly and simply. Most builders request training from lenders to cover FHA, VA, and conventional loan programs. Figures 4-11 and 4-12 illustrate a consumer financing worksheet and a form for calculating the real cost of home ownership. Depending upon the number and complexity of financing options and the new employee's background, training sessions in financing may require up to several hours.

Purchase Documents. Writing purchase documents may require up to a full day of training depending upon the background of the sales employee and the extent of sales responsibility for consumer selections and document processing. Training usually covers the following documents:

- purchase agreement
- contingent sale of home agreement
- special addendum forms
- order for standard options
- construction change order
- order for decorator selection
- order for cancellation of purchase
- warranty, truth-in-lending, disclosure statements, and other legal documents.

Contract Administration Orientation. The extent of this orientation will depend on whether the builder uses a central contract administrator or assigns this function directly to the sales staff. In either case, new salespersons should receive training on their specific responsibilities for contract administration and processing as well as information on responsibility delegated to others.

Settlement Procedures. Finally, settlement procedures, which vary according to local laws and customs, must be established. Orientation and training should cover the following:

- Settlement coordination, responsibility, and procedures
- Responsibility for new home orientation
- Key disbursement and occupancy
- Post move-in courtesy call
- Approvals for pre-settlement furniture storage
- Occupancy
- Preparation of warranty documents

Figure 4-11. Consumer Financing Worksheet

Ownership Analysis

A Personal Statement for _____

1. Total Investment   _____
2. Less: Initial Investment   _____
3. Amount Financed   _____
4. Monthly Principal and Interest (%)   _____
5. Real Estate Taxes (estimated)   _____
6. Homeowner's Assessment   _____
7. Insurance   _____
8. Private Mortgage Insurance   _____
9. Total Monthly Investment   _____

Type of Financing _____
Percentage of Total Investment _____

Salesperson _____ Date _____

Figure 4-12. The Real Cost of Homeownership

Price:	$ _____	Interest Rate	_____
Initial Investment	$ _____	Number of Dependents	_____
Loan Balance	$ _____	Estimated Annual Deductible Interest	$ _____
Monthly Investment (P&I)	$ _____	Estimated Annual Deductible Taxes	$ _____
Total Monthly Investment (PITI)	$ _____	Total Annual Deduction	$ _____
		Estimated Tax Bracket	_____

Before Home Purchase

1. Gross Income $ _____
   Less: Adjustments to $ _____
   Income
2. Equals: Adjusted Gross $ _____
   Income
3. Itemized Deductions $ _____
   Less: Exclusion $ _____
   Equals: Net Deduction

            $ _____

   Complete line 3 only if you currently itemize deductions. If you do not currently itemize, transfer adjusted gross income to line 4 and proceed.

4. Taxable Income $ _____
   Less: Dependent Deduction $ _____
5. Equals: Net Taxable Income $ _____
6. Federal Income Tax (Tables) $ _____

After Home Purchase

7. Gross Income $ _____
   Less: Adjustments to $ _____
   Income
8. Equals: Adjusted Gross $ _____
   Income
9. Itemized Deductions $ _____
   Less: Exclusion $ _____
   Equals: Net Deduction $ _____
   Plus: Annual Interest and $ _____
   Taxes
   Equals: New Net
   Deduction $ _____
10. Taxable Income $ _____
    Less: Dependent $ _____
    Deduction
11. Equals: Net Taxable Income $ _____
12. Federal Income Tax (Tables) $ _____

Figure 4-12. The Real Cost of Homeownership (continued)

Real Cost of Ownership

13. Total Monthly Investment $ _____
    (PITI)
14. Tax Savings First Year (6-12) $ _____
15. Tax Savings Per Month $ _____
    (divided by 12)
16. Equals: Net Monthly Cost $ _____
    (13-15)
17. New Tax Bracket   _____ %

Gain From Owning

18. Today's Purchase Price $ _____
19. Times Estimated Annual % $ _____ %
    Appreciation
20. Equals Estimated Annual $ _____
    Appreciation
21. Estimated Monthly Appreciation (divided by 12) $ _____
22. Estimated Monthly Net Cost of Home $ _____
    Ownership (16-21)

Chapter Five

Selling New Homes: The Success Formula

This chapter is addressed specifically to the builder's sales team—both salespersons and sales directors. The Success Formula For Selling New Homes is a comprehensive training program that defines the keys to effective sales and their use in unlocking doors that lead to proven sales success. It is a success formula that will produce increasing sales through diligent application and improvement. Using this formula, salespersons will discover capacities, strengths, talents, and abilities that may previously have gone unused or underused. The emphasis is on discovering individual potential strengths and developing them, leading to a more vital, creative, satisfying, and productive selling career.

This chapter presents the Success Formula for Selling New Homes in four major sections:

- The Professional Salesperson
- The Critical Path to Successful Selling
- Proven Sales Techniques
- Personal Priorities

The Professional Salesperson

The vast majority of new home salespersons do not acquire specialized knowledge through intensive education and training. These salespersons are not professionals. Professional salespersons consistently upgrade their skills, developing and constantly improving their professional confidence and expertise in the art and science of selling.

Controlling the Selling Process
Characteristics of the professional salesperson are apparent from the manner in which she or he handles and controls the selling process.

Success is contingent upon gaining and maintaining control of oral, written, and visual communications and making subsequent modifications to these communications according to prospect reactions. The sales professional thus controls the selling process by doing the following:

- Putting forth his or her best communication.
- Carefully recording the reaction.
- Adjusting communications in response to this reaction.
- Following up with even better communications.

This process is repeated as often as necessary to achieve the sale objective.

Self-Control. Effective control of the selling process requires internal self-control before attempting to control communications with the prospect. Both types of control involve improving internal and external actions through continuous learning experiences. Like a thermostat that activates a heating system toward a preset objective, the sales professional tunes his or her mental thermometer to the prospect's receptive temperature and adjusts his or her actions to modify that temperature toward the sale objective.

Successful Selling Communications. Sales communications should build a solid platform of confidence in the prospect's mind. Communications between a salesperson and a prospect must penetrate the normal forces of confusion that can distort the transfer of thoughts or ideas from one person to another. Signals transmitted by oral, written, graphic, gesture, and odor media are subject to these unknown forces of confusion, inhibiting mutual understanding between prospect and salesperson. Therefore, the professional salesperson speaks with great care and listens with even greater care and attention.

Salespersons should avoid the use of any words or phrases that might instill fear or discomfort and therefore slow the emotional purchasing pace. The impact of common selling words and phrases is exemplified by the list in Figure 5-1. The words in the left-hand column are common expressions in the real estate industry that sales professionals avoid in favor of the more appealing words in the right-hand column.

Prospect Reactions. Coupled with an initial understanding of a prospect's needs and preferences, prospect reactions are the keys to successful motivation. Constant sensitivity to prospect reactions allows the salesperson to respond immediately with actions designed to create new appointments, be-backs, and purchasers. The following three rules are vital to success:

- STOP communicating in order to receive vital prospect feedback.
- LOOK at the prospect's non-verbal signals for reaction messages.

Figure 5-1. Professional Words and Phrases

I. Professional Words and Phrases:

Non-Professional	Professional
project	community
unit	home/residence
buyer	purchaser
contract	purchase and sale agreement
deposit	initial investment
down payment	initial investment
monthly payment	monthly investment
sign (i.e. signature)	approve
execute	approve
condo	condominium home/residence
deal	opportunity
afford	how much do you want to invest?
lot	homesite
flat	Florida plan
townhouse	California plan
	charm price
premium	inexpensive
cheap	own
buy	get involved
sell	

II. Power Words:

Non-Professional	Professional
entry	gallery/foyer/sense of arrival
living room	formal/grand room
family room	informal/leisure/entertainment room
sliding glass door	indoor/outdoor partition
dining room	formal/elegant
kitchen	stepsaver/gourmet
eating area: kitchen	good morning room
master bedroom	owner suite/adult/luxury
upstairs bedrooms	quiet area/sleeping
bathroom	bathing salon/pamper room
toilets	water closets/commodes
double sinks	his and hers
designer tubs	love tubs
double closets	talk in terms of benefits/10 hanging garments per foot.
	designer
upgrade bathtubs	year-round wardrobe area
large closet	summer kitchen
built-in barbecue	motor court
parking lot	pedestrian paths
sidewalks	outdoor entertainment area
patio/balcony	

- LISTEN carefully to the prospect for verbal signals upon which to design response communications directing the prospect toward the appointment or sale objective.

Body Language. Understanding non-verbal gestures or body language is an asset when analyzing and selling prospects. With few exceptions, people will communicate their inner feelings through non-verbal gestures. If verbal communication is consistent with emotions and gestures, a person is likely to be telling the truth. The gestures and interpretations shown in Figure 5-2 should be recognized and used to advantage in every selling situation.

Prospect Control

Figure 3-8 illustrated a sample prospect card to be completed for each prospect immediately after every contact with that prospect. The prospect should never be requested to complete this card, since they usually have no particular interest in providing information. Many of them may feel annoyed when asked to fill out this type of card in order to view models. Smart salespersons never ask a prospect to fill out or sign any form except the signature line on a purchase agreement. He or she obtains information for the prospect card by simply showing friendly interest while making the presentation and keeping a few notes on the sales organizer carried in one arm.

Prospect Profiles

There are many different prospect profile types. The salesperson must quickly identify personality types in order to be truly successful. The following represents the more important types:

- *Ego-Centered Personality*

    Trait: Is very forceful. Knows everything.
    Strategy: Salesperson must be strong and try to be agreeable while pointing out all the benefits. Compliment this type.

- *Price-Conscious Personality*

    Trait: Uses logic rather than emotion.
    Strategy: Sell company, quality, benefits, and warranties.

- *Status Symbol Personality*

    Trait: Tries to impress salesperson with personal belongings. Wants the biggest and best.
    Strategy: Deep qualify this person—could be a phony. Quote highest-priced home and ask if it is within their price range. Show the best lots and use snob appeal.

- *Individualist*

    Trait: This person wears unusual clothes, drives odd cars. Likes to be different.

Figure 5-2. Specific Non-Verbal Gestures and Their Interpretation

Openness Posture:

- Open hands held out front
- Hands in back of head
- Unbuttoned coat
- Uncrossed legs
- Soft smiles
- Hands relaxed

Fear/Defensiveness Posture:

- Legs crossed at ankles
- Hand over mouth
- Perspiration on inside of hands
- Little or no direct eye contact
- Cupping nose with hand
- Buttoned coat
- Arms crossed over chest
- Hands clasped together behind back
- Fists clenched
- Narrowing eyelids
- Closed tight mouth
- Speech very low
- Hands in pockets

Action Posture:

- Hands on hips
- Sitting down/leaning forward
- Sitting on edge of chair
- Clear eye contact

Disinterest/Boredom Posture:

- Leg over chair
- Legs crossed/pointed away
- Eyes constantly rubbed
- Eyes out of focus
- Leg in constant motion
- No direct answers
- Constantly cleaning self

Interest Posture:

- Finger on temple
- Chin in palm of hand

- Legs crossed pointed toward
- Direct eye contact
- Firm handshake
- Eyes wide open
- Legs uncrossed/relaxed
- Leaning forward
- Chin stroking

Surprise Posture:

- Eyebrow raised
- Mouth open
- Eyes wide open
- Hand on heart

Authoritative Posture:

- Narrowed eyelids
- Loud voice
- Extra strong handshake
- Hitting hand with palm
- Moving very close
- Thumb gesture
- Cigar smoking
- Hand on person's arm
- Straddling a chair

Decision Posture:

- Hands in prayerful stance
- Finger pointing to brain
- Chair pulled close to table
- Direct responses
- Legs relaxed
- Hand on chin
- Positive agreement/shaking of head
- Voice clear and steady

Evaluation Posture:

- Cleaning or filling a pipe
- Cleaning glasses
- Pacing back and forth
- Hand on nose/eyes closed

Strategy: Discuss privacy lots (maybe a corner). Show the most contemporary plan.

- *Averageperson*

    Trait: Has a family and interested in neighborhood. Wants a house with good utility.

    Strategy: Discuss the school system if good. Discuss parks and recreation. Emphasize emotion.

- *Loud/Friendly*

    Trait: Likes everything. This person says yes to every question.

    Strategy: Watch out! This person is in most cases insecure and may not be truthful. Be jovial and laugh with him or her but, after each joke, get back on the critical path of selling. Work on specific answers.

Sales Mistakes

Among real estate salespersons of all personalities and levels of experience, there are common sales mistakes that should be actively avoided. The following list offers ten of the worst offenders:

- Relying on sales aids to inform and sell prospects.
- Neglecting up-front probing.
- Preliminary qualifying.
- Assuming prospect is familiar with the development.
- Not adjusting presentation to the individual.
- Ignoring model demonstration.
- Presenting too many choices.
- Forgetting to stress urgency.
- Failing to ask for the sale.
- Burdening the customer with the task of follow-up.

The Critical Path to Successful Selling

The Critical Path To Successful Selling is a step-by-step formula for guiding a prospect from initial introduction through ownership to the generation of referrals. As illustrated in Figure 5-3, the path consists of four sequential phases, each of which is climaxed by a critical event, or objective, achieved by controlling the selling process through a programmed series of prospect activities. The purpose of the Critical Path To Successful Selling is to specify the shortest series of essential activities and events leading to successful sales. Rigorous adherence to this path will result in optimal use of time with each prospect.

The underlying principle of this critical path method is to control the relationship with the prospect toward eventual purchase by limiting discussion to critical activities and resulting events. Extraneous activ-

Figure 5-3. Critical Path to Successful Selling

INTRODUCTION	DEMONSTRATION	FINALIZATION	CONTINUATION

73

ities, such as extended discussions of mutual friends, politics, religion, or sick relatives, are to be avoided or immediately redirected back to critical path activities.

The Critical Path To Successful Selling consists of a series of activities and events in four sequential phases:

- Introduction
- Demonstration
- Finalization
- Continuation

The length of time required to direct a prospect through the critical path will vary depending on the size and complexity of each development—but no less than one hour or more than two hours, on average. The salesperson must plan to spend this amount of time to ensure an effective sales presentation.

Phase One: Introduction

Greet to Win. Salespersons must sell themselves to the prospect, usually within the first five minutes, before attempting to sell any product. Therefore, the crucial first impression and initial information exchange must be carefully planned to ensure a solid basis for the selling process. The initial greeting is equally important whether in person, by telephone, or by mail. Salespersons should begin to build trust and establish a rapport immediately, identifying themselves to the prospects and getting the prospect's name. When greeting to win, successful salespeople should

- be on their feet,
- have a good attitude,
- wear a genuine smile, and
- be cordial and pleasant at all times.

Qualifying for Efficiency. This is a strategic dialogue through which the salesperson determines the non-financial qualifications of the potential prospect for homes in this community (Figure 5-4). Consumer responses provide the salesperson with a basis for prospect determination. If the person is not a qualified prospect, then a polite exit from the sales process is required.

If the person is a qualified prospect, the salesperson must first decide if an immediate close is possible. If so, the thing to do is to simply sit down and write the purchase agreement and move to Phase Three of the critical path: Finalization (p. 79). In most cases, however, an immediate close will not be possible, and the salesperson will proceed immediately to Phase Two.

Figure 5-4. Qualify for Efficiency

- Is this your first visit to _____?
- (Source) May I ask how you heard about _____?
- May I ask how many are in your family?
- Would you prefer a two or three bedroom?
- Will you be taking advantage of our excellent financing plans?
- How soon do you intend to purchase?
- Do you presently own a home or rent?
- Will you need to sell your present home?
- May I ask where you are living now?
- How long at your present home?
- What size home are you considering?
- Are you planning a move in the near future?
- How long have you been looking?
- Why are you looking?
- How soon had you anticipated making a move into a new home?
- How much time do you have today?
- What new homes have you seen so far since you have been looking?
- Have you seen anything you like?
- May I ask what appeals to you most?
- Our price range is _____ to _____. Is that the price range you had in mind?

Phase Two: Demonstration

Selective Area Orientation. An effective salesperson must have detailed knowledge of the area surrounding the subject property and selectively apply this knowledge to the specific needs and interests of the qualified prospect. For example, if meeting with a young couple with school-age children, a salesperson can draw upon an earlier visit to area schools in addressing the prospects' specific needs. Of course, if the prospects are single persons or empty-nesters, their interests will require selection of other area benefits. For example, a single person might be interested in local recreation facilities and health or social clubs. Empty-nesters may have questions about upmarket recreation facilities as well as houses of worship and social activities. Appendix A shows a sample area profile form that can be helpful in compiling pertinent information.

Effective Community Orientation. Orienting prospects to the development community requires that the salesperson adapt to the interests and needs of each prospect—an art requiring a thorough understanding of developer plans and construction programs. A community profile form is shown in Figure 5-5. It is also essential that the optimum way to tour the community be planned in advance.

Figure 5-5. Community Profile Form

Benefits of Living in Your Community/Neighborhood

I. General
    1. Name of Community: _____
    2. Location: Street Address: _____
       Town or City: _____
       County: _____ State: _____
    3. Mailing Address: Street or P.O. Box: _____
       Town or City: _____
       State: _____ Zip Code: _____
    4. Developer: _____
    5. Builder: _____
       Street Address: _____
       Town or City: _____ State: _____
       Zip Code: _____ Telephone: _____
    6. Interior Designer: _____
    7. Sales Agent or Broker (if applicable): _____
       Street Address _____
       Town or City: _____ State: _____
       Zip Code: _____ Telephone: _____
    8. Sales Director: _____
       Sales Office Tel.: _____ Model Tel.: _____
       Residential Tel.: _____
    9. Salesperson: _____ Residential Tel. _____
       Salesperson: _____ Residential Tel. _____
       Salesperson: _____ Residential Tel. _____

II. General Community Data
    1. Number of Homes in Community: _____
    2. Date Community Opened or Will Be Open for Sales: _____
    3. Estimated Date Community Will Be Sold Out: _____
    4. Price Range of Homes: $ _____ to $ _____
    5. Number of Models Featured in Sales Area: _____

III. Community Location Characteristics
     _____
     _____
     _____
     _____

Figure 5-5. Community Profile Form (continued)

IV. **Historical Background of Property**

Does the land on which this community is going to be built have any historical, cultural or picturesque story?

_____ Yes _____ No. If yes, please describe briefly, or where information about property can be obtained:

_____

_____

_____

V. **Community Improvements**

What improvements will be installed and paid for by builder, utility, or town prior to occupancy by buyers?

_____

_____

_____

_____

_____

VI. **Community Amenities**

List and describe ALL amenities included in the community: _____

_____

_____

_____

VII. **Negative Factors**

List and describe any negative factors about the community: _____

_____

Optimum Products Demonstration. This process requires total knowledge of the builder's new homes, which may include use of a product profile form (Appendix B). Every design and construction element is a potential selling feature, and every feature must constitute a special benefit for this particular prospect.

The optimum method to tour each model must be carefully planned in advance, as illustrated in the sample in Figure 5-6. A model home should be demonstrated from the outside in, beginning at the front of the house and pointing out features such as roofing, landscaping (if applicable), and siding materials. As the tour moves into the home, the salesperson should keep in mind the following:

● The group should go through one room at a time, with the salesperson pointing out all the features and benefits in these rooms to build even greater perceived value in the product.

Figure 5-6. Professional Product Demonstration

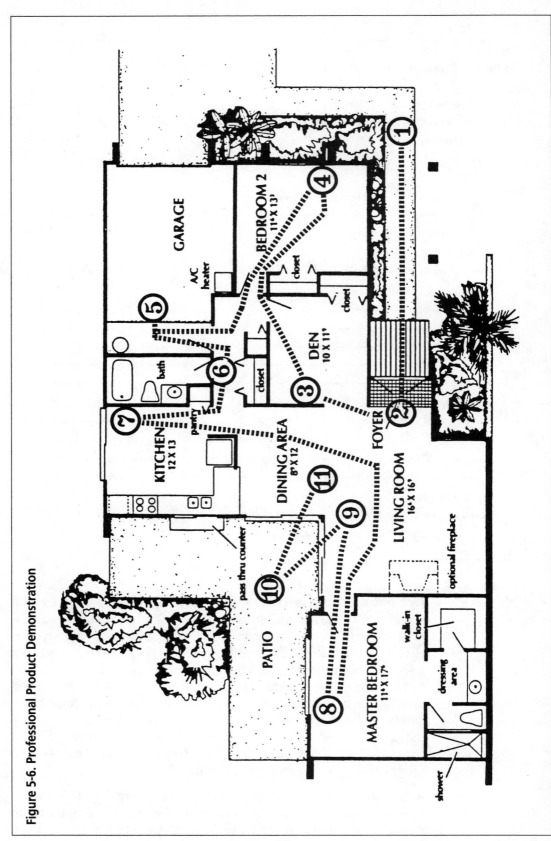

- It is always effective to have all the lights on in a model home.
- Window treatments that cut down on natural light and obstruct views should be avoided.
- The tour should be carefully planned to end up in the most dramatic portion of the house.

Upon completion of the three Demonstration activities, the salesperson must determine if the prospect is adequately informed about the area, community, and products. This determination is based upon continued questioning of the prospect throughout each of these activities.

Phase Three: Finalization

Reduce to Writing. Real estate is not sold by oral agreement. Written agreements can only be prepared adequately by sitting down with the prospect and reducing relevant purchase details to writing. This activity involves motivating prospects to the table and documenting key details to clarify all outstanding issues before purchase.

The primary issue at this point usually is monetary. Ownership financial details must be clearly analyzed for each prospect on an ownership analysis form (Figure 5-7).

Close, Close, Close. Obviously, closing the sale cannot be overemphasized. The close is the primary objective of the selling process and all other activities are secondary to it. The salesperson should keep in mind the following points:

- With a proper sales presentation, the salesperson has earned the right to ask for an order.
- The successful salesperson should be prepared to close at any location.
- After a successful sales presentation, the customer is in a position to make a decision and should be asked for an order.

Unfortunately, it is the rare salesperson who uses even the most fundamental closing technique—the urgency/fear-of-loss close. For example: "Why don't we go ahead and start the paperwork on your new home in order to have you in by _____ ?" (specific date). Or, "Why don't we go ahead and start the paperwork today to ensure that you will get the price we are quoting to you today?" Fear of loss of interest rate and location motivates buyers and should be used by *every* salesperson. Other specific closing techniques are found in "Proven Sales Techniques" on pp. 81-92.

Phase Four: Continuation

Follow-Up: Purchasers. If a purchase agreement is signed, the salesperson should immediately initiate follow-up activities to ensure formal ownership and eventual referrals. A sale is not consummated until the legal closing takes place, and the common onset of "buyer's

Figure 5-7. Ownership Analysis Form

A Personal Statement for _____

1. Sales Price of Home $ _____
2. Initial Investment $ _____
3. Loan Amount $ _____
4. _____ Years At _____%

Monthly Investment

5. Monthly payment for principal and interest $ _____
6. Monthly deposit for taxes (approximately)   + $ _____
7. Monthly deposit for insurance (approximately)   + $ _____
8. Monthly payment for homeowner association
   dues, etc.   + $ _____
9. **Total Monthly Payment**   = $ _____

Deductible Items for Income Tax Purposes

10. First month interest $ _____
11. Monthly tax deposit   + $ _____
12. Total   = $ _____
13. Total Monthly Payment $ _____
14. Less Deduction (28% of Line 12)   − $ _____   (monthly tax savings)
15. **Real Monthly Payment**   = $ _____

Economic Cost

                                                                  Equity
16. Line 5 minus line 10 $ _____   Gained Monthly
17. Real monthly payment $ _____
18. Less equity gained monthly $ _____
19. **Actual Monthly Costs** $ _____

remorse" can send any deal into limbo. Specified follow-up procedures during this period should include mortgage approval, color selection, and inclusion on the builder's public relations and promotions mailing list. The salesperson must accept primary responsibility for ensuring that each purchaser becomes a happy owner. In addition to the thank-you letter, move-in gift, and personal visit, the Prospect Control System (p. 29) should ensure life-long contact referral potential from each owner.

Follow-Up: Non-Buyer/Be-Back. When the selling objective is not achieved, follow-up must be initiated to create a "be-back." Follow-up relies upon daily use of the Prospect Control System. The salesperson knows that the be-back is the strongest prospect, and constant contact by telephone, mail, and in person is required to generate them. The successful salesperson does not burden a prospect with the task of follow-up but rather assumes full responsibility for follow-up with a telephone response within 48 hours and a continuing series of mail and telephone communications. Salespeople should continue follow-up efforts until prospects—as the saying goes—"buy or die."

Proven Sales Techniques

The following sales techniques have proven effective in controlling prospect communications from initial contact through on-site appointment to closing the sale. Specific communication control techniques for telephone, mailings, and personal contact are addressed first, followed by self-prospecting—the sales professional's primary means of generating new prospects. Techniques also are presented for answering objections, improving individual communication control skills through organized role playing, and closing the sale.

Incoming Telephone Calls

Salespersons should first realize that the only thing they can sell over the telephone is an appointment. However, the telephone ranks second only to face-to-face contact as a means of achieving those appointments. As illustrated in Figure 5-8, the average potential for setting appointments by telephone is one call out of every twenty, compared to only one appointment for every seventy-five personal letters mailed.

There are three basic types of incoming calls:

- new inquiries
- call-backs from prior prospects
- information and thank-you calls

New Inquiries. Incoming inquiry calls should be carefully planned communications, as illustrated in Figure 5-9. Salespersons should always identify themselves, ask for the name of the person calling, and begin a "mini-critical-path" to qualify the caller's needs and create a sense of urgency.

Call-Backs. A call-back from a prior prospect is a top priority call that should result in an appointment. Salespersons should follow the latter part of the new inquiry telephone technique summarized in Figure 5-9.

Information and Thank-You Calls. Information and thank-you calls require friendly and efficient response but no special technique.

Outgoing Telephone Calls

There are also three types of relevant outgoing calls:

- calls to potential prospects
- follow-ups with prior prospects
- follow-ups with purchasers or owners

When making any outgoing call, the salesperson should do the following:

- Set aside a block of time.
- Review the prospect control card and any previous meetings with the prospect.
- Plan the dialogue.
- Never allow the phone to ring more than four times.

All three types of outgoing calls are guided by the model dialogue in Figure 5-10.

Figure 5-8. Appointment Potential

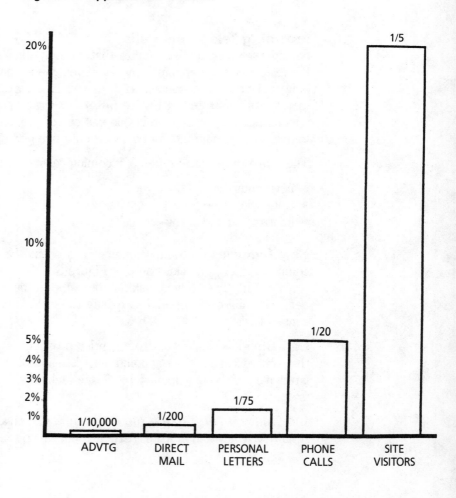

Figure 5-9. Model Dialogue: Incoming Telephone Calls

Answer telephone:

"It's a beautiful day at ___(community name)___ . May I help you?"

Introduction:

"My name is ___(salesperson)___ . May I ask yours, please?"

- "Thank you, Mr. (or Mrs.) ___(prospect)___ . How did you hear about ___(community)___ ?"
- "We offer two, three, and four bedroom homes. How large a home do you need?"*
- "May I ask how many will reside in your new home?"
- "Mr. ___(prospect)___ , how soon will you be needing your new home?"
- "Great! Our price range at ___(community)___ is from (low) to (high). Is that the price range you had in mind?"
- "Mr. ___(prospect)___ , ___(builder)___ takes great pride in offering our homebuyer the best and very latest financing plan available."
- "Would it be possible for you and ___(prospect)___ to come preview our several models at ___(community)___ and also let me tailor a financing plan to suit your needs. Would this afternoon or evening be better—3:45 or 4:45 be more convenient?"

Close:

- "Thank you, Mr. ___(prospect)___ . I know you will be as enthusiastic about our home as the many families who already live the ___(builder)___ way."
- "I'm looking forward to meeting at ___(community and time)___ . Goodbye!"

*Answer to square footage question: "I'm glad you asked—evidently square footage is important to you. Our homes start at (lowest square footage) and up. How many square feet were you interested in?"

Figure 5-10. Model Dialogue: Outgoing Telephone Calls

Identify yourself and community:

- "Hello, this is ___(salesperson)___ at ___(community name)___ ."

Convenience:

- "Have I caught you at an inconvenient time?"
- (If yes) "I'm terribly sorry, I'll call again. Thank you. Goodbye (hang up)."

Benefit:

- (Provide one beneficial reason to purchaser for your call).

Appointment:

- (The "Which" technique) "Which would you prefer, Friday evening or Saturday morning?"

Close:

- (Confirm) "I'm looking forward to meeting at ___(community and time)___ . Goodbye!" (hang up)

Rapid Response Mailing

This communication technique includes three types of mailings as described below:

Direct Mail. Direct mail is a form of printed advertising—flyers, letters, postcards, brochures—with a projectable rate of return. Whenever possible, advertising agency specialists in copywriting and graphics should handle these tasks, with a direct mail firm coordinating all bulk mailings. Unprofessional mass mailings usually are not cost-effective.

Personal Notes. While not a substitute for telephone calls, personal notes can be used as effective support communications (Figure 5-11). The best ones are always in personal handwriting, including the envelope addresses. The two envelopes in Figure 5-12 show the clear contrast between effective personal communications and "junk mail."

Collateral Information. Collateral mailings are customarily mailed as a substitute for the more difficult but far more effective personal notes. These mailings—often of sales brochures—are not an adequate substitute for effective personal communication and can inhibit the selling process by providing sufficient information for a potential prospect to reach a decision without a salesperson's guidance. In short, uncontrolled mailing of sales brochures is an expensive and inefficient use of sales team time.

Self-Prospecting

This sales technique is practiced by truly professional salespersons. Rather than relying solely upon advertising and promotion to generate walk-in traffic, the professional salesperson generates appointments through self-prospecting and diligent follow-up procedures, converting a high percentage of their prospects into purchasers through the Critical Path To Successful Selling.

Personal contacts constitute the most effective means of communication. While the confident salesperson does not immediately adopt a selling posture with every personal contact, he or she does exhibit the self-motivating confidence to search out prospects and convert them to satisfied purchasers through subtle means of communication. Such subtle means may include wearing a lapel pin or other small piece of jewelry indicating membership in a professional association, or perhaps manuevering conversations toward real estate topics to demonstrate expertise—without adopting a sales posture.

The first rule for successful self-prospecting is to eliminate fear, uncertainty, and doubt and become motivated in an efficient and effective fashion. In this sales context, efficiency is defined as the number of prospect contacts per day, per week, or per month. Effectiveness is the salesperson's success rate, measuring appointment/sales prog-

Figure 5-11. Sample Personal Note

> Dear Charlie and Trudy,
>
> I sincerely enjoyed meeting the two of you this past Sunday at The Sanctuary.
>
> Enclosed is a recent news article that may be of interest to you.
>
> If you have any questions, please do not hesitate to call. However, I will call you Friday the 15th between the hours of 5 and 7 pm.
>
> Sincerely,
> Gina Carlson
>
> P.S. The temperature is 68° and sunny.

ress toward pre-established annual, quarterly, monthly, or even weekly objectives.

Prospecting

Effective prospecting means searching out potential consumers and motivating them to become new home purchasers. Prospecting requires that salespersons consider their prospects in light of three basic questions:

- Who are they? Everyone is a potential prospect, either to purchase a home or to refer someone else to purchase. Narrowing the prospect search to groups with higher than average potential for purchasing a particular product is based upon identification of the characteristics of existing homeowners in this development and similar developments—family size, household income, head of household income, age, education, occupation, and previous residence type and location. These characteristics provide a profile of typical purchasers that serves to help identify additional high potential prospects. Changes in economic conditions, particularly financing interest rates, must be applied to adjust income criteria accordingly.

- Where are they? Prospects are everywhere: the grocery store, bank, civic clubs, even the service station. Of course, the process of locating prospects will vary with the particular character of each marketplace. For example, the personnel staffs of large companies are a valuable prospect resource for primary home sales professionals.
- How to attract them? To achieve the prospecting objective—onsite appointments—the salesperson must first avoid the common error of attempting to sell homes during off-site prospecting. The experienced professional recognizes the importance of communications

Figure 5-12. Sample Envelopes

that are neither too short nor too long but rather aimed at the crucial "success zone" time period for varying communications media. For example, this "success zone" for a telephone call may be only four to six minutes, while a personal contact might need ten to fifteen minutes to be successful.

In order to achieve the prospecting objective of scheduling an appointment, the high-performance salesperson programs communication to ensure constant feedback from the potential prospect through controlled dialogue. A common mistake of non-professionals is to dominate the communication—the sales professional is an astute listener as well as a verbal motivator.

The Positive Approach to Answering Objections

First, salespersons must understand that prospect objections constitute expressions of genuine interest. Second, the professional salesperson welcomes objections as signs of progress in the selling process—satisfactory resolution is often the final breakthrough to sale finalization.

The majority of all objections from new homes prospects are related to money, location, and size. The salesperson should anticipate these objections and be prepared to resolve them clearly, succinctly, and preferably on paper. Financial worksheets, amortization tables, and current financing information should stand at the ready for money issues. A locator map with pre-calculated distances and times to major community locations should be prepared for location issues. Interior and exterior space-planning features and benefits must be ready in response to size issues.

Consistent success at answering objections involves preparation for two distinct stages of the answering process:

- Initial response: includes a positive, receptive attitude and sympathetic and confidence-inspiring word selection.
- Dialogue: includes customized reply techniques (Figure 5-13).

Closing Techniques

While the number of closing techniques is great, there are several with which every real estate salesperson should be familiar:

Urgency. As mentioned earlier, every salesperson should use the sense of urgency to his or her advantage—starting school, beginning work, or ending a lease, for example.

Writing the Purchase and Sales Agreement. When a salesperson has achieved an affirmative, qualified prospect, the salesperson should start writing. With the contract already on the desk facing the purchaser, the salesperson should turn the document around and state: "I'm going to show you what the financing looks like." The salesperson

Figure 5-13. Common Sales Objections and Suggested Answers

Objection:	"I would have to let my husband (or wife) see it."
Answer:	"Fine. I will make up the agreement for you, and we will put in a clause that this is not effective until your spouse approves it. Why don't we take a deposit of $100 until this final approval?"
Objection:	"The taxes are too high."
Answer:	"Oh yes, that is true all over the country. But you can write it off. The taxes reflect the quality and value of the property." (Stress how fortunate they are to be able to buy such quality and be able to write it off. Also explain the residency requirement for homestead.)
Objection:	"Interest rates are too high."
Answer:	"I agree. However, our rates are competitive. You can wait, but prices will go much higher." (Show statistics.)
Objection:	"The bedroom is too small."
Answer:	"Fine, but consider the price, and I would like you to look at the huge size of (mention largest room in home or unit). That extra space was put in _____ _____ where most used."
Objection:	"This is $5,000 more than we wanted to pay."
Answer:	"Yes, but it is only $500 more down payment (usual 10 percent) and your monthly payment will only be $ _____ more per month." (Break it down into daily rate and stress the extra space and convenience for only $ _____ per day.)
Objection:	"We are not ready yet."
Answer:	(What is the prospect considering as to the best time? Search for the real reason.)
Objection:	"We want to think it over."
Answer:	"Folks, what exactly do you want to think over? You do like the location, do you not?" (Now go over all the points you noted (positives) while you were demonstrating and doing your trial closing. Write everything down and show it to your prospects. Tell them this is a checklist of their likes and dislikes. When you get to the bottom, ask them, "What do you have to think over?")
Objection:	"Are these laminate counter tops?" Or: "Are these ceramic counter tops?"
Answer:	"Yes, isn't that wonderful? With laminate, you just need to wipe them off with a damp cloth. And you won't have any cracks and cement falling out."
Answer:	"Yes, ceramic counter tops surely are quality."
Objection:	"There is no shower in the tub."
Answer:	(Give an example of how reasonable it is to install enclosure and know prices.)
Objection:	"Isn't that a fiberglass shower?"
Answer:	"Yes, it is a solid piece of construction and very modern and easy to maintain."
Objection:	"Do we have gas cooking?" Or: "Do we have electric cooking?"
Answer:	"Yes, and isn't it so very clean. And gas cooking costs less to operate."
Answer:	"Yes, and isn't it so very clean. It is found in all your better homes, and electric cooking has no pilot light to burn out."
Objection:	"There isn't a separate entry."
Answer:	"But the balance adds to the spacious (mention largest room), and it shows real economy because there is no wasted space."

Figure 5-13. Common Sales Objections and Suggested Answers (continued)

Objection: "But there isn't a dining room."

Answer: "Well, that is true, but we have a large family room that is used most of the time. And did you know that a formal dining room is used only 5-10 percent of the time?"

Objection: "There is too little wall space."

Answer: (Know your product. First find reason for use of room and then set in your own mind how you could arrange furniture *under* windows.)

Objection: "There isn't a family room."

Answer: "Yes, but look at this large ranch kitchen (or other example), your large living room, and the big backyard."

Objection: "Is this drywall?"

Answer: "Yes, and it is used throughout this area. Not only is it economical, but only one-half inch gives you the sound and fire resistance you need. The temperature is constant, and it will not crack."

Objection: "Isn't that a crack in the slab?"

Answer: (Agree) "This is normal because of the continuous run of the concrete with no separators."

Objection: "There isn't a dishwasher."

Answer: (Again, know the cost of a dishwasher and installation from local dealer and give this information as a positive to your prospects.)

Objection: "The economy goes down."

Answer: "Home values have consistently gone up in value through strikes, depressions, business cycles, and wars." (Get lists and statistics.)

Objection: "The payments are too high."

Answer: (Stress value of home—project through statistics.)

Objection: "But we would have to get a second loan."

Answer: "Yes, but look at the leverage you have. You would need a smaller down payment and would have a larger return in the end on invested capital."

Objection: "Please do not pressure us."

Answer: "I hope you do not mistake my enthusiasm for pressure."

Objection: "The house is too small."

Answer: (You know they cannot afford a larger home. Show them how comparable the price and balance will be and paint pictures that they can always step up to a larger home later. Stress rental vs. buying and the advantages of buying.)

Objection: "We do not want to sell our stock now."

Answer: "Fine, but you could use the stock as collateral to borrow enough for a minimum down payment."

Objection: "We have just started to look."

Answer: (Confirm what they have already agreed to. These are positives taken during your trial closings while demonstrating.) "It would just be an exercise in further looking. You are lucky because you found the home of your choice early." (Assume this is the best for them.)

should write up the contract, turn it around, and explain the items, always referring to the document as the "agreement to purchase." Finally, a pen should be offered to the prospect with a request for his or her approval.

Choice Location. "Making a decision on this particular home gives you the choicest location because we have just begun to sell."

View. "The prime consideration of this location is that you have a very special advantage in having a nice view. The view will also be a positive in your asking price should you ever resell this home."

Neighborhood Facilities. "Because of the schools and the large shopping mall being so close to this home, I feel it adds real value to your purchase now and in the future. Would you prefer to move in the first or the middle of next month?"

Paperwork Close. "You seem to really be positive about the home we just looked at; however, there are some lender requirements we must consider." (Salesperson hands them a credit application.) "Please fill out this credit application as best you can, and we'll see if it would be acceptable to the lenders." (Note: this technique should be employed if the prospects seem underqualified.)

Urgency of Inflation. "Material costs are going up every day." (Salesperson shows an article from a home-building industry publication or Department of Commerce.) "It is a fact that these homes will be more expensive just because of increased material costs. Why not freeze this home cost today by purchasing now? Would you like to invest 10 or 20 percent?"

Throw-In Extra. "We have been together for one hour. You like that large lot but seem to be worried about the costs involved in putting in a lawn and fencing. To help you out, we will include grass and fencing in your backyard. Would you like us to have that fence installed on the first or fifteenth of next month?"

Secluded Location. "The reason you really like this home is the seclusion. You're surrounded by a large fence and trees. This seems to be the number-one factor in your life-style. Would you prefer to close the sale by the end of next month or beginning of the next?"

Find the Reason. "Mr. and Mrs. Jones, you seem to really like the location, price, neighborhood, and financing, yet you find it difficult to make a decision. What is the *real reason* for hesitating? Maybe I can help you solve the problem." (Salesperson should serve as a counselor and be empathetic.)

Option to Purchase. With standing inventory, it is sometimes prudent to install a lease-option-to-buy program. When the prospect shows a definite reluctance to purchase, the salesperson can agree and suggest that it might be best to live in the house for a year with a lease and then have the option to purchase.

Out-of-Towner. A prospect is being transferred and is really impressed with the models. However, the spouse is not there. The salesperson should suggest that the prospect select a specific location and approve the sales agreement subject to the spouse's total approval. Salesperson should take only a minimum deposit, perhaps $100.

Competition Close. Salesperson admits the competitors are fine builders (salespersons should never be overly critical of another builder) and presents a sheet of all the positive advantages of purchasing this home, ignoring the competition if possible. Salesperson must know all strengths and weaknesses for this technique to be used effectively.

"Homes Aren't What They Were." "Yes, that's correct, we're building much better today. When you move into this home, you will find much greater energy savings than in your previous home. This is due to materials that are available now in order to cut your costs. Would you prefer purchasing the corner home or the one in the cul-de-sac?"

Time Decision. "You have stated you like the location, price, neighborhood; the only question I would like to ask is when would you like to move in, thirty or sixty days?"

Carpet Color Close. "You seem to really like this location." (Prospect is in inventory house.) "Let's see, you did say you liked the beige carpet, is that correct?" If prospect answers "yes," respond with: "When would you like us to install the carpet? The first or fifteenth of next month?" If the prospect answers, the salesperson should be quiet and begin writing as soon as possible.

Take Off the Pressure. If a salesperson has a husband and wife in a closing situation and the pressure seems to be increasing, the salesperson should get up and suggest that they reach their own decision. After ten or fifteen minutes, the salesperson should return and ask: "When did you decide to move in, on the first or the fifteenth?"

Prestige Purchase. "Mr. Jones, this home will suit your needs very well. It is on the golf course and has the spacious living room and dining area that will be important for all the entertaining you will be doing. I know you will be proud of the neighborhood."

Minimize the Decision. "I know this home will be $3,000 more than you expected, but if you figure that on a monthly basis, it is only about twenty-five dollars per month extra or a little more than seventy-five cents a day."

Follow-Up Appointment. The prospects cannot make a decision now. Salesperson should summarize all their positive reasons for purchasing and give them a filled-out purchase agreement, credit application, brochure, community information, and any other collateral material.

Role Playing

Role playing is a regular habit of successful sales professionals, helping them improve their sales skills. Practicing sales techniques on prospects is a potentially expensive approach to learning weaknesses—in the event a salesperson even receives enough feedback to understand what went wrong. Smart salespersons practice regularly with each other to strengthen techniques and detect weaknesses.

Rules for both seller and prospect behavior during role playing sessions must be defined in advance. First, clear objectives for each role playing session—defining prototype prospect and techniques to be tested—must be established. Next, open, objective criticism from observers must be encouraged within the parameters of positive assistance and a friendly environment. Salespersons may also wish to practice role playing alone, simply by practicing certain segments of the critical path until they feel fully comfortable with the techniques. Practicing in front of a mirror, perhaps with a tape recorder for later review, can also prove effective.

Personal Priorities

The pleasures of personal growth and development require effort, self-discipline, and a certain amount of pain. For the sales professional, the rewards are well worth the daily control and determination required to establish and implement priority objectives. Following are tested methods of efficient time and information management for the new homes salesperson, followed by guidelines for personal goal setting and evaluation. Daily adherence to these methods will result in improved sales and income performance.

Making Money Through Efficient Time Management

Sales success results from personal planning and programming to ensure concentration on key money-making activities. Personal planning and programming involves a series of five steps:

- Determination of objectives to be sought.
- Research to understand the problem.
- Discovery of alternative solutions.
- Choosing between alternatives (including the frequent choice of doing nothing).
- Detailed execution of the chosen alternative(s).

As previously described, the Prospect Control System provides a means for daily and monthly planning and programming. Alternate solutions for achieving appointments and sales must be formulated at the beginning of each day and the highest potential alternative selected for each prospect. This is followed by a program of prospect contacts throughout the day.

Sales professionals supplement the Prospect Control System with a calendar program guide or similar time organizational calendar to plan future activities and maintain evaluation notes on daily production.

Individual sales goals should be formally recorded on a standard form (Figure 3-4). Summary records of daily sales activity extracted from prospect cards are maintained on the daily sales activity form illustrated in Chapter Three.

The Sales Professional Organizer

The professional salesperson never relies solely upon memory for information in a selling situation. The ideal memory supplement is a sales professional organizer—a three-ring binder containing all relevant selling information in a format organized for easy reference. Many builders provide an attractive binder with imprinted logo.

Staying Ahead of the Competition

Since up-to-date knowledge of the competition is vital to sales success, the professional salesperson keeps a companion notebook to the sales professional organizer: the competition organizer. This binder contains product and selling information on competitive products—brochures, sales prices, financing plans, and personal evaluation data derived by shopping each competitor at least twice per year.

Personal Evaluation Guidelines

Personal guidelines help salespersons regularly determine their progress toward individual sales goals. Although sales volume and income earned are the ultimate annual criteria, weekly sales activities can be evaluated by the following four guidelines to gauge progress toward peak sales performance:

- Production: the number of prospect contacts (in comparison with individual goals) and the extent of selling time (relative to a 40-hour or 2400-minute week).
- Efficiency: time per onsite prospect (one to two hours), time per telephone prospect (should not exceed ten minutes to achieve an appointment), and time per mailing (should not exceed 15 minutes).
- Effectiveness: net sales (new sales minus cancellations) compared with individual goals.
- Conversion: net sales per number of inquiries compared with individual goals.

Conclusion

For the professional salesperson, success is measured in terms of satisfaction—both a lengthy list of satisfied customers and satisfying annual compensation. The foregoing components of the Success Formula for Selling New Homes constitute the key ingredients for achieving this success. However, accompanying these components must be those human traits by which individuals judge each other: honesty, integrity, loyalty, industry, and a genuine affection for others. The combination of these traits with Success Formula techniques is a winning one, generating satisfying and productive selling careers.

Chapter Six

Implementing a Broker Cooperation Program

The ultimate objective of every new home sales program is maximum sales with minimum expenditures of time and money. An organized program for sales through real estate brokers can contribute substantially toward this goal.

While the program outlined in this chapter is designed to be implemented in conjunction with an onsite sales staff for maximum potential sales, the builder or other staff person can coordinate if sufficient time is scheduled for the task. Of course, it is also possible to implement a broker cooperation program through a designated broker representing the builder, a particularly useful option for small-volume builders who may not maintain permanent model locations. Regardless of method, builders who have initiated and maintained aggressive cooperative programs with brokers and agents report that between 25 percent and 75 percent of their sales come from the general real estate community. It is not surprising, then, that increasing numbers of builders across the country are targeting broker sales programs as a top sales priority.

Program Objectives

The primary objectives of a broker cooperation program are as follows:

- To increase sales.
- To generate pre-qualified selling opportunities.
- To expand beyond an onsite sales staff through networking.

For a broker cooperation program to succeed, brokers must be treated as consumers. Not only are they potential purchasers themselves, but they also represent unlimited repeat business as agents for new home buyers.

The Builder-Broker Relationship

Historically, the relationship between builders and brokers has been uneasy and tentative. Each questions why cooperation is mutually beneficial and how to structure a program that fulfills both parties' needs. For any partnership to work, there must be mutual advantages. Therefore, the first step toward achieving cooperation is to develop mutual understanding of the potential benefits to each party. The second step is to understand the differences between the way each does business—such differences being the most common cause of misunderstanding and lack of cooperation.

Benefits for Brokers

Broker benefits from cooperative new home sales include the following:

- A broker cooperation program offers ease of sale, with the builder's sales staff qualifying prospects, demonstrating features and benefits, closing new home sales, processing documents, and arranging settlements.
- New home warranties provide a safer solution than a resale home for many purchasers.
- Special consumer financing is often available for new homes that is not available for resale homes.
- Consumers' special needs are hard to meet with resale homes; new homes can often be builder-equipped to satisfy such needs.

Benefits for Builders

Broker cooperation helps the builder achieve the overall goal of increased sales within a specified period and acceptable budget. The growing strength of the real estate sales community reflects the increasing effectiveness of its communications and business network. Because of the highly visible multiple listing services, guaranteed sale programs, relocation departments, and other consumer programs, many potential purchasers turn automatically to real estate brokers for assistance. Major advantages to the builder in broker cooperation include the following:

- Access to transferee buyers, who are likely to work through a broker when they arrive in a new community.
- Access to more move-up buyers, who often list their current residences with a real estate agency before purchasing a new home.
- Access to the multiple listing services, peer contacts, and networking.

Key Differences Between Brokers and Builders

Understanding the differences between real estate brokers and builders from a sales perspective is important to building a good working relationship. Based upon this understanding, bridges can be built between the two to facilitate cooperation. The following points may prove helpful in developing a better understanding of the builder-broker relationship:

- Real estate agents are married to their clients and must put them first, while builders are married to their products. This key difference colors nearly every aspect of the respective sales processes.
- Brokers control the sales process by building a close, lasting relationship with the client, serving as a counsel in the decision-making process. New home salespersons must greet, qualify, and gain control of the selling situation rapidly with each new prospect.
- By its very nature, a resale home purchase involves negotiation of price and terms. Conversely, a builder resembles a retailer in that prices are not normally negotiable because of fixed builder costs. A builder may offer special pricing, but only to meet specified sales objectives within the context of the overall sales program.
- Brokers sell the reality of existing homes in established neighborhoods, whereas new home salespersons sell the dream of what will be. Selling dreams requires special training, detailed knowledge of the builder's plans, and unwavering belief in the reality of the vision. Although brokers may acquire detailed product knowledge, their normal operating procedure of touring clients until the right home is identified precludes them from dedicating their efforts to a single builder's products.
- Purchase and settlement on an existing home takes relatively little time, while it may take six months or more to complete purchase of a new home started after a contract is accepted. Many brokers are not accustomed to working with consumers over protracted periods of time and/or waiting more than 60 to 90 days for their sales commissions.

Research: Finding the Top Brokers

Developing a targeted cooperative sales program requires research of local real estate sales data to target high-performance real estate brokers and agents. In the case of a broker cooperation program, accurate definition and identification of brokers is the best assurance of a successful program. Experience has shown that a small, select group of brokers—fewer than 20 percent—sells the vast majority of all real estate. For this reason, the builder needs to identify the area's most successful professionals and focus special attention on them.

It is also well known that each real estate broker's sales tend to concentrate in a small, well-known geographic area. These areas of concentrated sales are generally within a five-mile radius of the real estate firm's offices. Therefore, it is reasonable to begin targeting brokers within five miles of the builder's current sales location, expanding outward from the site in concentric circles.

Research objectives should focus on the development of three broker lists:

- General contact: an extensive list defining the "universe" without regard to the specific qualifications of either the firms or individuals identified. This list will be used for systematic or general communication.
- High achiever: a refined list identifying top-producing real estate firms and associates within reasonable proximity of the sales location. This list will be targeted for personalized contact and follow-up by builder salespersons (if applicable) and sales management.
- New licensee: a list of new licensees that can be targeted for new home sales training or other forms of special promotion.

Program Plan and Budget

A plan and budget must be prepared for any broker cooperation program. The following guidelines should help the builder in both planning and implementing these elements.

Planning for Broker Cooperation

When planning a cooperative arrangement, the builder returns to the Critical Path To Successful Selling, adapting it to the special needs of broker/builder cooperation. The key steps are summarized as follows:

- Introduction: includes identifying primary brokers, establishing contact with primary prospects, and qualifying each broker prospect for potential sales effectiveness.
- Demonstration: includes formal invitations for selected candidates to attend professional product demonstrations, where a builder representative specifies the advantages of membership in the cooperative broker program.
- Finalization: includes providing full assistance to cooperating brokers in finalizing each sale, as well as providing written prospect registration and protection procedures to ensure full broker confidence in the cooperative relationship. The builder should ensure brokers a level of compensation and incentives at least equal to regional industry standards.
- Continuation: includes recognizing each cooperative sale with a high-visibility gift and maintaining continuing personal and group contact follow-up with every member of the cooperative broker program.

Two of the most effective approaches for successful broker cooperation planning are described below:

Shotgun. The shotgun approach targets all licensed real estate brokers in the market area. Contacts are usually gained through broker wine-and-cheese parties held to introduce a new product or reintroduce an older product. Brokers can be contacted through direct mail as well as through messages through multiple listing services.

Rifle. The rifle approach identifies brokers within a two-mile radius of a site who continuously excel in selling houses in the builder's particular price range and are noted in the Million Dollar Circle. These brokers can easily be identified by checking with brokers. These top achievers should then be targeted for aggressive one-on-one contact.

Budget

Issues to be considered in budget preparation include the following:

- Broker commissions should be established equivalent to the prevailing selling commission in the area (in reality, one-half of the full commission). An optimum number of targeted sales should be defined in order to estimate the budget (for example, 50 percent of sales at a 3 percent compensation level would require an allocation of 1.5 percent of gross sales revenues for broker cooperation commissions).
- Brokers are independent businessmen. When given a choice between selling homes at higher or lower levels of compensation, they will prefer the higher compensation. A builder who discounts compensation to brokers is unlikely to achieve the sales objectives desired from a cooperative program.
- Onsite salespersons should always be paid the full onsite sales commission on cooperative broker sales in order to generate enthusiastic support for the program.
- Marketing expenditures should be allocated for special public relations, advertising, and printed materials for broker cooperation.
- Special incentive programs should be planned for brokers, including sales contests and contact awards.

Public Relations and Promotions

An aggressive public relations and promotions effort is the backbone of a successful broker cooperation program. Real estate professionals, like all other consumers, respond to special treatment and consideration. A public relations program directed at them should be double-edged—highly structured through specific programs, yet low-key in salespersons' personalized efforts.

It is a mistake to underestimate the sophistication of today's brokers. Gone are the days when "brokers always come if a builder serves free food." Professional, high-achieving real estate professionals are more likely to visit a new home community today if the builder offers special educational seminars on new home construction (using builder's senior staff) or hires a sales expert to speak on sales techniques. Similarly, incentive programs are shifting from money toward other rewards that combine value with enjoyment.

Broker Contact and Follow-Up

Both the sales manager and salespersons should expect broker contacts and follow-up to be a part of each day's routine. The targeted list of high achievers in the real estate community should be distributed among the sales staff as the basis for a continuing program of personal contacts. Activities with brokers should be reported on daily sales activity forms (Figure 3-11) and monitored by sales management. Types of contact should be varied and include the following:

- Personal visits to brokers' offices.
- Handwritten thank-you notes for registering clients or for personal visits to the information center.
- Follow-up telephone calls encouraging visits to the information center and registration of prospective purchasers. These calls may also report on the progress of a sale.
- Hand-addressed and personalized letters conveying new information.
- Formal presentations at real estate company weekly sales meetings.
- "Tour Days" for local real estate companies to visit the site during their weekly office tours of newly listed properties.
- Explanation of the builder's program for customer service. This program should be sold as convincingly to real estate brokers as to consumers.

As in all prospecting activities, personal visits or telephone calls are more effective than written communications. Mail contacts should be used to reinforce personal contacts or to set a time and date for a follow-up visit or telephone call, rather than as a substitute for personal contacts.

Public Relations

In addition to general broker contact and follow-up, a systematic program of public relations should reinforce contacts with both high achievers and with the real estate community at large.

Program Components. Systematic public relations programs should include the following:

- Regular real estate agent newsletters containing articles on sales policies and procedures, special pricing, new products, individual brokers recognized for cooperative sales achievements, and special awards or honors given to brokers.
- Special onsite promotions including seasonal events (grand opening or holiday open house, for example) and special seminars (Understanding Blueprints, How to Demonstrate a New Home, or Understanding Construction Techniques).
- Special mailings announcing new sales incentive programs, new prices, or other timely sales information.

Preferred Broker Program. Many builders have found that a Preferred Broker Program helps target special sales opportunities, personal contacts, and frequent communications to a select group of brokers who have demonstrated an interest in cooperative new home selling. Enrollment in this preferred program usually requires attendance at a special training program that

- explains broker cooperation policies and procedures,
- provides an information center and model home tour, and
- reviews pricing and other information.

Participants in the Preferred Broker Program are targeted for other special treatment, including the following:

- Members-only special incentive programs or sales contests that enable participants to earn shopping sprees, vacation trips, or multiple-sales bonuses.
- Regularly scheduled breakfasts or luncheons for updating sales information.
- Seasonal "thank-you" events such as holiday parties or annual golf tournaments.
- Regular awards programs on a monthly, quarterly, or annual basis.
- Periodic educational seminars by recognized local and national experts on new home sales techniques or other appropriate topics.
- Framed certificates for membership in the Preferred Broker Program, attendance at educational seminars, and awards or honors for sales achievement.
- Special client registration procedures that ensure full compensation for telephone registrations, waive the time-limit for protection, or expedite providing information for prospect cards.

Promotions: Special Incentive Programs

All special incentive programs (whether targeted to preferred brokers or the real estate community at large) should be tied to specific sales objectives. Typically, a builder's objectives might be as follows:

- Develop pre-construction contracts.
- Speed sale of specific standing inventory.
- Increase the level of broker-generated consumer inquiries.
- Encourage multiple sales by individual brokers within a specified time period.

Incentive programs should make awards achievable and fun. Everyone likes to win, even if the prizes are small; therefore, it is better to have graduated award levels—such as those common in airline "frequent flyer" promotions—than to have a single grand prize that most cannot win.

First-level awards in an incentive program might include $100 gift certificates, candlelight dinners for two at a favorite local restaurant, or "Great Escape" hotel accommodations at a nearby vacation spot. Second-level awards could include travel and lodging to a regional resort area, golf clubs, or other sporting equipment. The final award level might offer foreign travel and lodging, cruise accommodations, or fine jewelry.

Since the objective of all incentive programs is to encourage maximum participation, some builders base awards on a point system that involves brokers in the promotion even before a sale is made. For example, increasing onsite consumer inquiries is a valid promotional objective. Recognizing this, brokers could accumulate points for their first visit to the information center and tour of the models. Additional points could be given for each consumer registration. A proportionately larger number of points could be awarded for each purchase agreement written during the contest period. When awards are achieved through the point system, the broker is given the choice of redeeming the prize upon attaining the first award level, or continuing to accumulate points for prizes at the next award level.

Advertising

In the normal course of their business, real estate brokers are avid readers of weekend classifed and display advertising. More than any other potential consumers, they can be reached reliably by builder advertising. The builder should therefore address this segment of the market both through regular consumer advertising and special programs:

- All consumer advertising should include a message on broker cooperation (for example, "Broker Sales Welcome" or "Full Cooperation with Brokers").
- Special ads should be placed periodically to thank brokers for their support and/or congratulate individuals for recent sales.
- Ads should be placed in local Board of REALTORS® publications and real estate franchise company newsletters. Ads should contain information on registering clients, in addition to general consumer information. Ads can also thank or honor local participating real estate firms.
- A program of direct mail should also be implemented to reach the targeted broker audience. Lists prepared for the general real estate community, high-achievers, and new licensees should be used for direct mail.

Product Merchandising

Product merchandising includes everything consumers experience once they arrive at the information center. As consumers, brokers will respond to each element of the builder's onsite merchandising—from entry signage to designer home interiors. The primary difference between brokers and other consumers is their need for information beyond that normally provided.

While brokers do need additional sales information, dissemination of this information must remain carefully controlled. When salespersons not skilled in new home sales give detailed product information to consumers, the consumer often makes a negative buying decision without visiting the information center. Therefore, individual brokers or real estate companies should not be provided with an inventory of marketing and sales brochures. Since the function of marketing and prospecting is to attract inquiries to the site, where professional new home salespersons can convert inquiries into sales, this type of brochure distribution would obviously be counterproductive.

In keeping with the philosophy of treating brokers as repeat customers, they should be given a complete sales brochure upon each visit to the information center. Distributed in this way, the information in the sales brochure is used by the broker to support information provided to the consumer in the planned presentation.

In addition, at the first or subsequent visits to the information center, brokers should be given the facts about the broker cooperation program that they will need to work with consumers and the builder's sales staff. This information generally takes the form of a special insert (Figure 6-1) in the general sales brochure or a simple policies and procedures manual (see below).

Organization

The basis for a successful broker cooperation program is a set of written policies and procedures that are simple, clear, and fair to all parties. Policies and procedures should address the typical broker's concerns in the sale of a new home: ease and fairness of client registration procedures; timely payment of commissions; and protection of the broker/client relationship, which culminates in payment of the commission. All policies and procedures should be clearly set out in a broker cooperation policies and procedures manual available for distribution to all interested real estate associates. Issues to be covered in the manual are addressed below:

Registration Procedures

Registration procedures should be in writing and should be distributed to brokers at every opportunity. They should include a broker registration card (Figure 6-2).

Broker associates registering a client are usually protected from onsite sales for 30 or 60 days following registration. Though some builders provide protection from other brokers registering the same prospect, this policy can be detrimental to builder sales potential; it is recommended that policies state that the builder will honor the most

---

Figure 6-1. Sample Broker Fact Sheet

BROKER PARTICIPATION IS EASY AT
(Name of Community)

(Name of community) places a high value on the professionalism and mutual trust we have with our broker friends throughout the area. In a very real sense, our success depends on you and your willingness to work with us.

To prevent misunderstandings and to help assure a smooth working relationship on behalf of your prospects, we suggest the following procedure:

1. Always register in our permanent broker participation program by filling out the registration form on your customer's first visit.

2. We offer a 3 percent cooperative brokerage commission to any registered cooperative broker.

3. Naturally, we have no control over a customer changing brokers. Should that occur, we will register both brokers. In order to earn a commission, the broker or broker associate must be the "procuring cause" of the sale.

4. Once the sale is made, our salesperson will follow through on necessary details to consummate the closing on your behalf—including mortgage financing and closing arrangements.

5. All contracts must be written on our standard forms as required by local legal standards.

6. Escrow deposits will be paid to (name of builder), the developer of (name and community). Commissions will be paid in full at closing, unless otherwise agreed upon in writing.

---

recent registration. When a double registration occurs, the builder's salesperson should inform the first broker that another has registered the client, nullifying the original registration. The exception to this rule is a consumer's declaration in the "disclosure of agent" clause of a purchase agreement naming the first agent as the representative.

Commissions
Payment of commissions is usually established in similar fashion to commissions paid to onsite sales staff, including the two-stage commission payment schedule for pre-construction sales described in Chapter Two.

Client Protection
Client protection is a vital issue for broker associates. Most brokers should be sufficiently reassured that they are properly protected by the following policies:

- The builder's onsite salespersons are prohibited from selling resale properties.
- The onsite salesperson receives full compensation, even on cooperative broker sales.

Figure 6-2. Broker Registration Card

Date: Expiration Date:

Client Information: Broker Information:

Name	Name
Address	Firm
City, State, ZIP	Address
Telephone	City, State, ZIP
	Business Telephone
	Home Telephone

For Office Use Only:

Registration Expires (date): _____

Registration Extended to (date): _____

General _____ H.A. _____ P.B. _____ N.L. _____

Personal _____ Mail _____ Telephone _____

Confirmation Required? _____ Confirmation Date _____

Registration Validated Through Prospect Files _____

    Valid Registration Confirmed (date) _____

    Prior Broker Registration Noted _____

    Letter to Previous Broker (date) _____

    Prior Consumer Registration Noted _____

H.A.: High Achiever
P.B.: Preferred Broker
N.L.: New Licensee

Because of the importance of client protection to the real estate community, a letter confirming a client registration should be sent to a broker within 48 hours of the initial registration visit. Figure 6-3 is a sample letter to be used for this purpose. Again, the exception to this rule is a consumer's declaration in the "disclosure of agent" clause of a purchase contract naming the first agent as the representative.

Figure 6-3. Sample Letter Confirming a Broker/Client Registration

Date

Sam Jones
Citywide Home Sales
500 Evergreen Way
Anytown, USA 54321

Dear Sam:

This letter will confirm your representation of William R. and Jeannette Smith in any purchase of a Quality Home at Countryside occurring prior to July 1, 19____. Should you desire to extend the 60-day period for which the Smiths are registered as your clients, you may do so by calling Countryside Homes at (817) 555-4321, at which time a new letter of confirmation will be issued.

Thank you for registering the Smiths at our Information Center. I am looking forward to working with you and your clients over the coming weeks. If you have any questions about our homes and procedures, please do not hesitate to call on me.

Sincerely,

Beth Brown
Quality Homes, Inc.
Countryside

Selling Operations

Each visit by a real estate broker to the information center represents a selling opportunity. The salesperson must therefore rapidly assess the purpose of the visit and qualify the broker in order to determine the appropriate planned presentation. There are four primary types of broker visits:

- Preview visits: the broker receives a planned presentation demonstrating the features and benefits of the area, community, products, and builder. This presentation also includes explanation of cooperative broker policies and procedures and the Preferred Broker Program.

- Preferred broker registration: encouraged for all brokers who visit the site and take sufficient time for the above presentations.
- Broker/consumer visits: planned presentations by the onsite salesperson to ensure control of the selling process.
- Unaccompanied consumer visits: the arrival of a consumer at the information center who has been previously registered by a broker either in person or by telephone. The consumer should be asked to confirm the broker referral.

Once a broker's client has been registered at the information center, regular follow-up contacts should be made with both consumer and broker:

- Forty-eight hours after visit, telephone calls should be placed to both the consumer and the agent to encourage a return visit.
- Prospect card and regular follow-up should be implemented according to the policies and procedures in Chapter Three.
- Post-sale follow-up with the referring broker should be maintained throughout the period between the sale and the closing.
- After the move-in, the onsite salesperson should visit the broker's office to thank the broker for the cooperative sale and to offer assurance that the new owner's customer service and other needs will be promptly met.

Consumer Surveys

Survey results can enhance the credibility of a broker cooperation program. Therefore, positive results from consumer surveys should be shared with area brokers. They have a vested interest in the ultimate satisfaction of each client, as well as a need to be reassured that cooperative new home sales will be a profitable and pleasant experience. In addition, brokers can be surveyed as valued repeat consumers whose attitudes and satisfaction are very important to the sales performance of the community. Figure 6-4 illustrates a sample survey that can be sent to each broker after the settlement of a cooperative sale.

Figure 6-4. Broker Survey

Thank you for taking the time to complete this survey. We are committed to making the sales of our homes by brokers a rewarding and enjoyable experience. We highly value your opinion because of your most recent experience with us.

1. How would you rate the quality and value of (name of builder) homes in comparison with other new homes in the area?

   _____ Excellent   Please comment: _____

   _____ Good   _____

   _____ Fair   _____

   _____ Poor   _____

2. During your most recent sale at (name of builder) homes, was our sales staff cooperative and courteous?

   _____ Very   _____ Somewhat   _____ Not At All

3. Did our salesperson provide you and your client with information on:

	Yes	No	Uncertain
Alternative design plans:	____	____	____
Customizing alternatives:	____	____	____
Optional features:	____	____	____
Color selections:	____	____	____
Financing alternatives:	____	____	____
Exterior materials/color choices:	____	____	____
Closing costs:	____	____	____
Community advantages:	____	____	____
Construction methods:	____	____	____
Important area facilities:	____	____	____
Customer service program and warranties:	____	____	____
Mortgage application/processing procedures:	____	____	____

4. In the time between the purchase and settlement, did our salesperson:

	Yes	No	Uncertain
Communicate regularly with your purchaser:	____	____	____
Communicate regularly with you:	____	____	____
Respond promptly and courteously to requests:	____	____	____
Update you on the progress of the sale:	____	____	____
Prepare all sale-related documents:	____	____	____
Make all arrangements for settlement:	____	____	____

5. Overall, how would you rate your level of satisfaction with the (name of builder) cooperative sale experience recently completed?

   _____ Very Satisfied   Please comment _____

   _____ Satisfied   _____

   _____ Somewhat Satisfied _____

   _____ Unsatisfied   _____

   _____ Uncertain How I Feel _____

6. What could we do to make showing and selling our homes a more pleasant and productive experience for you? Please comment:

   _____

   _____

   _____

THANK YOUR FOR HELPING US SELL A (NAME OF BUILDER) HOME

Chapter Seven

Ensuring Sales Through Purchaser Satisfaction

Repeat business is every builder's best source of future sales. The number of referral and repeat sales obtained will be in direct proportion to the effectiveness of the builder's customer service program. The builder's program must therefore ensure the prompt, courteous resolution of problems that may arise during the sales process and after settlement or occupancy.

Purchaser satisfaction is an implied or expressed objective of every building company—extending from initial land acquisition and development through architectural design and construction to final sale, closing, and post-sale activities. Although the purchase of a new home is often an emotional decision, consumers support and rationalize their decision through their confidence in both the product and the builder's service and warranty programs—programs that enhance housing value and protect the consumer's investment. Thus, in addition to solving consumer problems, a customer service program is a powerful sales tool in the hands of professional salespersons.

Organizing a Customer Service Department

The quality of a building company's customer service department can mean the success or failure of a purchaser satisfaction program. The organization and structure of this department will vary depending upon the company's size, location(s), and products. For some builders, the program may include a substantial budget, additional staff, and capital investment in office space, overhead, and material inventory. Small-volume builders who cannot afford a separate staff person for customer service must perform this essential function personally. However, these smaller builders can also reap the benefits of effective customer service through dedicated application of customer service principles.* In either case, the payback from customer service activities can be equally real and far greater than the costs in time and money. Builders with well-established and successful customer service and overall satisfaction programs report over 40 percent of all inquiries and sales from homeowner referrals.

Assessing Staff Requirements

The number of staff and field personnel required in the customer service department will vary according to the company's volume. In smaller operations, one congenial, part-time employee may handle customer service work. Larger companies generally include a director, secretarial support, and one or more customer service representatives. The director of the customer service department most commonly reports directly to the builder or company president, ensuring the independence and integrity of the department in its relationships with both consumers and other departments. Subcontractor work may be requested under individual agreements on quality of workmanship and materials, or under a separate contract for additional work.

Customer Service and Quality Control

Builders often discover that quality control improves when customer service procedures are implemented. In the long run, it is less costly to do it right the first time than to repair, replace, adjust, or reinstall. While some delays in delivery can be overcome without damaging overall purchaser satisfaction, chronic late delivery or lengthy postponements will almost inevitably lead to widespread dissatisfaction.

Establishing Objectives

The roots of satisfaction, or dissatisfaction, are found at every point of contact with the consumer. Therefore, a customer service program must be supported throughout the building company by every employee and subcontractor. Specifically, achieving purchaser satisfaction requires a company-wide commitment to developing realistic consumer expectations; fulfilling or exceeding the builder's commitments to the consumer; and communicating clearly, honestly, and responsively with the consumer. Leadership must come from the top and be sustained and reinforced until the desired objectives are attained.

The following discussion addresses the role of purchaser satisfaction from first contact with the purchaser to an effective customer service program and beyond. The objective of every builder should be to achieve 100 percent happy owners who generate other happy owners.

---

*See *Customer Service for Home Builders* (Washington, D.C.: National Association of Home Builders, 1988).

Establishing Expectations in the Sales Process

During the planned sales presentation, the salesperson should concentrate on the following purchaser satisfaction objectives:

- Introducing the builder's programs for quality assurance and customer service.
- Building perceived value.
- Differentiating the builder from the competition.

Discussion of the customer service program should occur early in the presentation through demonstration of wall graphic displays in the information center. This introduction should include a brief description of the builder's warranty programs and their relationship to lasting quality and value. Collateral materials supporting these programs are often provided during the presentation or included as text and inserts in the community's marketing brochure. Some builders create a special logo, such as a Texas builder who markets customer service as "Gold Triangle Service" with the three legs of the triangle representing key program ingredients: Dependable, Prompt, Professional.

At the time the sale is consummated, the salesperson should familiarize the purchaser with customer service procedures in greater detail. The purposes of this introduction are to educate the consumer, develop mutual understanding, and establish appropriate expectations concerning the builder's obligations to the consumer.

Warranties

At the time the purchase agreement is signed, the salesperson should explain each warranty in detail, providing collateral materials as appropriate. This presentation should present the structural warranty; the builder's warranty of materials and workmanship; and warranties on appliances, heating and cooling systems, and other mechanical equipment in the home.

Purchaser Contact Log

Regular verbal communications are essential to purchaser satisfaction, and weekly contact with the purchaser should be maintained from the time of purchase through closing. Many salespersons maintain a purchaser contact log containing notes on subjects discussed by telephone or in person, as well as information transmitted and decisions or requests received. Such a log accomplishes several objectives:

- The log assists the sales director in answering questions or solving problems when the salesperson is not present.
- The log permits the transaction to be reassigned if the salesperson is transferred or employment is terminated.
- The log constitutes written documentation of communications in the event of later dispute or litigation.

- The log assures the sales director that the salesperson is in contact with the purchaser on a regular basis.

Consumer Site Visits

Consumer visits to the site can often be controlled through simple policies designed to minimize injuries and work disruptions. The salesperson should explain these policies to all consumers. Typical policies may include the following:

- A salesperson or the construction supervisor must accompany all consumers.
- Children under the age of fifteen must be under the control of the parent at all times to reduce accidents and injuries.
- New owner visits are restricted to specified days or hours, typically late afternoons or weekends.

The consumer should be treated with unflagging courtesy by every employee, including all subcontractors and their employees. Common courtesy to visitors prohibits drinking, profanity, or otherwise offensive behavior on the building site. Subcontractors and their employees should be informed of the builder's policies for onsite visits, and field superintendents should be responsible for enforcing these policies.

Documenting and Processing Agreements

Miscommunication and lack of mutual understandings are primary causes of purchaser dissatisfaction, often leading to complaints about misrepresentation or broken verbal promises. For this reason, all agreements should be reduced to writing in the purchase agreement and addenda, change orders, decorator selections, and contracts for construction options.

Many problems can be avoided at the outset by preparing well-written documents and establishing logical procedures. When problems develop because of ambiguity in a written agreement, the form or the procedures related to that form should be modified to eliminate potential problems in future transactions.

Inappropriate Expectations. Inappropriate consumer expectations can result from confusion between standard features, available options, and unavailable model decoration items. Well-trained salespersons can usually ease consumer confusion on these issues better than special signs that can be moved, lost, or overlooked. However, what a salesperson clearly states and what a consumer equally clearly hears frequently turn out to be different. Figure 7-1 shows a form for separately listing both construction options available for purchase and decorator features not available in production homes. This form, signed at the time of purchase, is a useful reference in the event of a later dispute. In addition, it is vital to use standard forms for construction options, change orders, and customer selections. By reducing all de-

Figure 7-1. Sample Description: Model Home Options and Decorator Features

MODEL: The Mariner

COMMUNITY: Glen Cove

The following features included in our furnished model are available as special options. Your salesperson will be happy to help you order any of these special features from Quality Homes, Inc.:

- Furnace-assisted heat pump
- Crown molding in living room, dining room
- Chair rail in dining room
- Luxury carpet and pad
- Ceramic tile floors in entry, baths
- Hardwood floors in living room, dining room

The following items included in our furnished model are special decorator features and are not available:

- Refrigerator, washer, dryer
- Furnishings
- Mirrored wall in entry
- Built-in cabinets and bookshelves in den
- Special light fixtures in kitchen, dining room
- Wallpaper
- Decorator paint colors

Purchaser is also aware that the security system and dead-bolt locks are not included in the purchase and that landscaping will consist of a seeded lawn.

Homebuyer	Date
Homebuyer	Date
Salesperson	Date

cision areas to signed documents, unnecessary misunderstandings can be avoided and purchaser satisfaction increased.

Document Control and Processing. Efficient control and processing of pertinent documents within a building company is an essential ingredient to purchaser satisfaction. Typically, the sales department originates most of the sales documents, with the construction department generating weekly summaries on the progress of each home. In addition, the purchasing or estimating department normally originates price lists for construction options and individual estimates for change orders.

Figure 7-2 describes the typical flow of documents between departments and company management. All sales, purchasing, or estimating documents described above require management review and approval and are usually transmitted to management offices within twenty-four hours of completion. A forty-eight-hour period for review, approval, and circulation back to appropriate departments is typical in many companies.

Before the New Home Orientation

The consumer's first impression of the completed home is a lasting impression. Immediately prior to orientation, each home should be thoroughly cleaned and readied for placement of furniture, dishes, and other household items. Finishing touches should also be given to the home's exterior and the surrounding site.

Many builders use a detailed quality inspection checklist to ensure that the home is complete, correct, and clean prior to closing. This inspection is usually conducted by customer service staff or, alternately, a team consisting of the field superintendent and the salesperson. The resulting written list of construction defects should be provided to the field superintendent for immediate correction. Usually, three to five days are allowed for completion of corrections, depending

Figure 7-2. Document Flow Chart

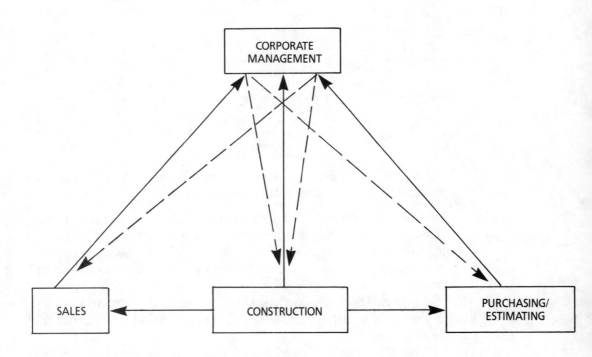

—— DIRECT FLOW OF DOCUMENTS

– – – INDIRECT FLOW OF DOCUMENTS FOLLOWING REVIEW AND APPROVAL

upon the policies of the company. Such corrections should be completed prior to the New Home Orientation. When this deadline cannot be met, the builder should inform the purchaser of corrections required and offer an approximate date for completion.

The New Home Orientation

The importance of repositioning the "customer walk-through inspection" as a New Home Orientation becomes obvious as settlement approaches. Consumers mistakenly assume that the walk-through inspection is their final opportunity to spot construction defects when, in fact, a builder providing a one-year warranty on materials and workmanship backed up by a customer service department is fully prepared to correct defects at any time during this period. On the other hand, proper consumer education prepares new owners to approach orientation and settlement with appropriate and reasonable expectations. They will be familiar with the builder's quality inspection, customer service procedures, and the functions and purposes of the New Home Orientation. They will therefore be less liable to expect problems and more confident about their new home—and the builder.

Purposes of the New Home Orientation

The New Home Orientation has several purposes, all of which should be explained to the consumer during the planned sales presentation:

- Familiarizing the new owner with the operation of the home's major systems and appliances.
- Providing information on the care and maintenance of appliances, floor coverings, counter tops, bathroom fixtures, and other features.
- Reducing customer service calls by teaching consumers how to check for the most common causes of problems or malfunctions.
- Providing instructions for the care and maintenance of materials used in the home's construction, which may extend the life and beauty of easily damaged components and reduce accidental damage not covered by the builder.
- Explaining the consumer's maintenance responsibilities, the builder's warranty responsibilities, and the differences between the two.
- Providing information about special construction features, including weatherization and energy efficiency, or about special construction conditions, such as soil instability and appropriate compensation measures.
- Verifying that the home is complete and ready for owner occupancy.

The "inspection" purpose of the New Home Orientation should be positioned as secondary to the purpose of providing information and assistance that the consumer will need to occupy the home in security and comfort.

Responsibility for the New Home Orientation

Builders frequently assign responsibility for the New Home Orientation to the director of customer service (if applicable) to establish post-sale consistency. Because effective communication and interpersonal skills are essential during orientation and later consumer contacts, the following recommendations on selecting and training a customer service director or other builder representative should be considered:

- The individual should possess substantial interpersonal or selling skills. These can be enhanced through assistance from the sales director and special training programs as needed.
- Orientation may begin as a joint meeting among the new owner, builder representative, and salesperson. After general topics have been covered and the representative and purchaser have been introduced, the salesperson can politely exit, leaving the technical presentation to the representative. This procedure facilitates the transfer of contact from the salesperson to the customer service department.
- If a salesperson has reason to expect unusual problems during an orientation, a special strategy should be planned. In this case, either the sales director or salesperson should be present for the orientation.

All sales staff should be familiar with the planned presentation delivered at the New Home Orientation. This familiarity is crucial if sales personnel are to establish appropriate expectations during the sales process. In addition, their periodic review and evaluation of orientation can improve the presentation.

Controlling the Orientation

Controlling the New Home Orientation helps ensure its effectiveness. Control should be exerted in subtle ways without eliminating positive interaction with the consumer:

- Before each orientation, the new owners should be given a preprinted orientation checklist organized according to the presentation. Many builders send out this checklist in advance, along with a letter of welcome to reinforce the purposes of orientation. Purchasers should be asked to follow along, ensuring that each item is covered thoroughly.
- The builder representative should pause before entering the home and briefly outline the orientation's many purposes. Once inside the home, the rules of social courtesy will cause most consumers to follow, rather than lead.
- All builder representatives conducting orientations should practice techniques for diverting questions to the appropriate point in the presentation. When an issue arises that will be addressed later, consumers should be politely asked to hold the question for later discussion.

At the conclusion of orientation, the builder representative and the consumer should sign the checklist, with copies to each acknowledging their agreement.

Handling Problems

Despite careful preparation and planning, problems may arise during a New Home Orientation that jeopardize the scheduled settlement. Every effort should be made to overcome these problems during the meeting and clear the way to a closing. Unresolved problems tend to escalate and can be more difficult to overcome if not addressed promptly.

Serious problems that arise at orientation usually result from one of two causes: unrealistic expectations on the part of the consumer, or genuine defects in the home that may have been overlooked or caused by recent damage or vandalism. If problems are a result of unrealistic expectations, each item should be discussed according to the standards of local or regional building codes, Home Owners Warranty, or other warranty companies. Use of independent, third-party standards for acceptable quality of workmanship and materials will lend credibility to the builder's position.

If major defects are the cause of the conflict, the best policy is to correct them prior to closing and occupancy. Every effort should be made to minimize the consumer's inconvenience due to the delay in settlement date. Once the home is reinspected for deficient items, the customer should sign an affidavit of acceptable completion (Figure 7-3).

Settlement

Coordinating the settlement of a new home can be a traumatic and emotional time for a consumer. The best remedy for pre-settlement jitters is frequent and supportive communications from the builder's representatives. Careful preparation for the closing is essential. Every effort should be made to avoid rushed, "Chinese fire-drill" closings that telescope several weeks of work into days or hours.

By settlement day, the consumer should be familiar and comfortable with the builder's programs for satisfaction and service. Nevertheless, consumers are prey to uncertainties, concerns, and fears that are not necessarily realistic or proportionate to the situation. As settlement approaches, levels of concern and uncertainty increase. Support and assistance from the sales staff can help jittery purchasers overcome these problems.

The salesperson should make settlement arrangements and inform the consumer about what will occur before, during, and after settlement. Preparations should include scheduling the New Home Orientation and settlement, confirming that all documents are properly prepared, and providing information for planning the move. Many builders

Figure 7-3. Home Purchaser's Affidavit of Acceptable Completion

Name _____ Date _____

Address _____ Lot/block _____

I have this date completed a thorough introduction of the above identified property and the house erected thereon with a representative of the Company _____, and hereby certify that it is complete.

The quality of workmanship and material is acceptable to me. I understand that the Company does not intend to do any further work on my home concerning items that I determine, at a later date, to be unacceptable in terms of quality and workmanship. I understand that the signing of this statement in no way relieves the Company of its obligations, under any warranties, concerning functioning of the equipment or any structural failures that may show up at a later date.

Please note:

Signing this affidavit is in no way to be construed as a condition of this sale. It is a method to help insure to the management of the Company that our policy of completing your home before you move in is being followed up by our employees to assure you of this benefit.

_____

Purchaser   Date

_____

Purchaser   Date

_____

Builder

By: _____

provide a moving checklist with instructions for ordering essential services, contacting local schools or government agencies, and obtaining local emergency service (Figure 7-4).

Scheduling Customer Service

A series of return service calls to each home is unnecessarily costly and time-consuming to a building company. For this reason, many builders provide service at scheduled intervals during the first year after settlement. Homeowners are asked to keep a record of minor problems for correction at these regular intervals.

Regardless of interval service policies, service for emergency problems should be available at all times. The customer service department should have a telephone line dedicated to incoming emergency service calls; this line should be connected to an answering machine or answering service for evening or weekend use.

Figure 7-4. Sample Moving Checklist

1. **30-Day Preparations:**

   _____ Sort and inventory household goods

   _____ Obtain moving cost estimates

   _____ Obtain moving cartons or other supplies

   _____ Make any required travel arrangements

   _____ Notify correspondents and magazine subscriptions of change of address

   _____ Arrange transfer of medical and dental records

   _____ Arrange transfer of automobile and other insurance

   _____ Arrange transfer of school records

   _____ Close or transfer charge accounts

2. **7-Day Preparations:**

   _____ Arrange disconnection of services: telephone, water and sewer, trash collection, telephone, long distance calling service, gas, electrical, newspaper, cleaning, lawn care, cable television, etc.

   _____ Transfer bank accounts, if necessary

   _____ Arrange disconnection and servicing of heavy appliances, special antennas, etc.

   Arrange for connection of new services:

   _____ Electricity (State P & L, phone)

   _____ Gas (State Gas Service, phone)

   _____ Trash Collection (City Services, phone)

   _____ Water and sewer (County Services, phone)

   _____ Telephone (State Bell, phone)

   _____ Newspaper (Morning News, phone)

   _____ Cable Television (CableVision, phone)

   _____ Other:

3. **On Moving Day:**

   _____ Check all utility connections

   _____ Check for mail being held at post office (address)

   _____ Complete school registration process

4. **Schools, Government, and Emergency Services:**

   Neighborhood schools serving the community are:

       Lincoln Elementary School (phone)

       Jefferson Junior High (phone)

       Washington Senior High (phone)

   City Information (phone)

   County Information (phone)

   Emergency Numbers:

       Gas (phone)

       Electricity (phone)

       Water (phone)

       County General Hospital (phone)

       Ambulance (phone)

       Paramedics (phone)

       Fire (phone)

Each incoming call should be recorded on an emergency service request form. All requests from homeowners for routine service should be submitted in writing on a standard request form. Many builders provide this request form for the first service interval during the New Home Orientation to reinforce builder interest in purchaser satisfaction. An effective customer service department maintains careful records on services received and acknowledges receipt of requests with a letter or pre-printed postcard. Work orders are used to authorize corrections. The homeowner signs each work order as completed, to be followed by a mailed confirmation to the homeowner that the work has been completed.

How to Say No

The ability to say "no" when the situation requires is essential for all customer service personnel. Despite a desire to satisfy every consumer, a builder must treat all owners consistently and fairly. To help reduce friction caused by denying service requests, the builder or customer service representative should do the following:

- Obtain complete and reliable information before reaching a decision. The consumer is not necessarily the best source of information; inspection of the property should usually be made before denying requests.
- Prepare an "unreasonable" consumer for "no." If an exception is made in approving a request item, the owner should be told that repairs of this type are not usually covered under the warranty. Advise the owner that, while an exception will be granted in this case, similar requests will not be honored at a later time.
- When a "no" is required, do not temporize. Saying "maybe," or "I'll have to get the builder's opinion" simply undermines the staff person's authority and increases disappointment when the request is ultimately denied. Allowing days, weeks, or even months to elapse before saying "no" raises false hopes in the consumer and makes the negative decision harder to accept.
- Provide advice on steps the homeowners can take to correct a problem themselves. Often the cost of a repair is only part of the issue to homeowners. They may be equally concerned about their own inability to correct the problem. Offering technical advice and assistance provides a partial solution.
- Keep in mind that a homeowner's flash-point may be considerably lower than a builder's. In rare instances, a homeowner may become abusive when confronted with a "no." If this occurs, it is best to terminate the conversation calmly and give the consumer an opportunity to regain his or her composure. This can be done by saying, "I understand that you are very upset right now, so I am going to terminate this conversation (telephone call) and get back together with you around four this afternoon." Under no circumstances should any staff person respond to anger with anger.

Creative Approaches to Purchaser Satisfaction

Builders throughout the country have enhanced purchaser satisfaction and customer service programs by implementing creative new solutions such as the following:

Literature Distribution

Written instructions for new home care and maintenance, such as a new home manual* or series of pamphlets, often resolve many consumer complaints. Using individual pamphlets for specific parts or functions of the home makes it easier to replace outdated information— for example, when a new material or appliance is substituted.

Warranty Service Voucher System

This voluntary program has proven successful for many builders. Under a typical voucher program, an account is opened by the builder in the new owner's name with a specified deposit, perhaps $200. The new owner is then given ten printed vouchers for $20 each and a list of the names and telephone numbers of subcontractors. The consumer places calls for service directly to the subcontractor, paying at the rate of one voucher per hour. Subcontractors then redeem the vouchers for builder payment. Payments are deducted from the new owner's customer service bank account.

At the end of the warranty service period, the owners sign a release verifying that they are fully satisfied with their new home and have no further requests to make of the builder. Any remaining balance in the customer service account is then given to the owner, including interest.

The results of such a voucher program can be extraordinary. New owners perform their own simple service repairs, calls to subcontractors are infrequent, customer service staff can be reduced, and new owners are delighted to be saving their own money. The program is easy to budget, inexpensive to staff, and simple to explain.

Subliminal Selling

While many builders unknowingly engage in subliminal selling every day, all builders should actively use this customer service/sales tool. For example, many builders equip their customer service vehicles with identification of their function. When not in use, service vehicles are parked in sight of the information center. Similarly, customer service representatives are provided with shirts and/or jackets displaying customer service identification. Each time a consumer spots these obvious

---

*See *Your New Home and How to Take Care of It* (Washington, D.C.: National Association of Home Builders, 1987).

indications of customer service activity in the community and around the information center, the purchaser satisfaction message is reinforced.

Good Neighbor Program

This program has been developed to generate referrals through purchaser satisfaction. A typical Good Neighbor Program incorporates the following key elements:

- A program director—The Good Neighbor—is responsible for creating and coordinating all program activities, which have as their ultimate purpose the generation of owner referrals.
- In addition to ongoing activities planned for existing residents, the Good Neighbor Program provides activities for the new purchaser at each of the four stages in the purchase cycle: purchase agreement signing, closing, move-in, and the 30-45 day period following move-in.
- An annual survey, coordinated by the program director, tests the effectiveness of the Good Neighbor Program. Results from this survey are used annually to improve the program.

MONITOR

Chapter Eight

Profiting from Consumer Analysis

"Learn from experience" is an old adage with direct and profitable application for small-volume builders. Completed products, marketing communications, and sales presentations are all experiments that are constantly subjected to consumer testing. Consumer response to each of these "experiments" constitutes the initial measure of a builder's success.

Observation and analysis of consumer response is the *Monitor* function. A builder must have current information on the acceptance of product offerings, as well as on the cost effectiveness of marketing and sales activities. This is the essential feedback process: comparing actual results with marketing and sales plan objectives and revealing plan modifications for improving performance.

Two excellent and economical sources of information on improving builder management decisions are 1) consumers who visit the information center and 2) those consumers who subsequently purchase a new home. The purchaser is the builder's outstanding expert on purchaser needs and preferences and can also provide valuable feedback on the entire purchase experience.

Consumer Surveys for Small-Volume Builders

Builders of all sizes receive a continuing stream of consumer opinions during the course of work and social functions. However, scattered, ill-organized comments are of limited value in planning and evaluation. While a more reliable opinion sample would prove immensely more useful, such seemingly sophisticated market research may initially seem beyond the budget limitations of most small-volume builders. However, this need not be the case.

While consumer survey applications may appear sufficiently complex and costly enough to discourage most small-volume builders, the consumer opinions they generate are too valuable to ignore. Therefore, the paramount issue for the small-volume builder is how to acquire valid consumer opinions on products and marketing functions at low cost. The answer for many builders is to confine survey questionnaires to current new home purchasers and limit the involvement of market research analysts—if used at all—to the critical areas of tabulation and analysis of responses, tasks often requiring specialized computer programs and an experienced analyst. Thus, the following discussion focuses on a new owner survey program, followed by a summary of other cost-effective survey applications.

Surveying New Home Buyers

Surveys come in a wide variety of types, sizes, and costs. They can be conducted in person, by telephone, or by mail; structured or unstructured; direct or indirect. Surveys can be focused on individuals or groups. Typically, unstructured interviewing is conducted in organized discussion or "focus groups."

New Owner Survey Program

To get the most from every survey dollar, small-volume builders should concentrate on new residents as a continuing source of information, including valuable insights into the following:

- housing needs
- levels of satisfaction
- product features and designs
- marketing effectiveness
- sales presentation performance

Their opinions are particularly valuable within thirty to forty-five days after purchase. A second follow-up survey conducted about one year after purchase provides a useful comparison with the initial follow-up survey, particularly if the second questionnaire emanates from an independent source, such as a market research company. Thus, the new owner follow-up survey has dual purposes:

- Informs the new resident that the builder is vitally interested in purchaser satisfaction as well as opinions.
- Collects facts and opinions for management information and use.

The second survey has the primary purpose of collecting independent opinions from the residents without bias from those who might like to communicate directly with the builder on complaints or other issues.

Survey Design. The design of both of these surveys should be completed by professionals in accordance with the particular needs and circumstances of each builder. However, the initial design can normally be used for several years of questioning. Figure 8-1 presents a successful homeowners survey.

Surveying Procedures. Once surveys have been designed for both the 30-45-day new owner follow-up survey and the one-year survey, surveys should be distributed and analyzed as follows:

- A tickler file is established by week or month, extending over a two-year period. Survey packages—containing a survey questionnaire and cover letter from the builder or market research firm (if applicable), plus a stamped return envelope addressed to either the builder or market research organization (one-year survey)—are inserted into this file for each new owner at closing.
- A clerical person on the builder's staff is responsible for mailing the envelopes from the tickler file each week or month throughout the year.
- Responses from the 30-45-day survey are collected and submitted in bulk to the market research organization semi-annually or annually (annually for most small-volume builders with 50 or fewer sales) or maintained internally for tabulation and analysis with normal spreadsheet computer software. Responses from the one-year survey are similarly retained for tabulation and analysis annually.
- Computer tabulation and analysis of completed questionnaires normally requires one month, usually scheduled prior to completion of the annual marketing plan and budget—for example, questionnaire tabulation and analysis in November for plan and budget preparation in December of each year.

It is useful to complete the analysis of both surveys simultaneously to compare responses on similar types of questions. In addition, both types of information provide valuable input to the annual marketing plan and budget process.

Additional Consumer Survey Applications

In addition to the foregoing new owner survey program, builders employ a number of other survey programs. Each of these programs should be designed to meet the following requirements:

- Clearly stated survey objectives.
- A plan for securing reliable answers and cooperation from a representative sample of respondents, whether the data are collected from personal or telephone interviews, mail surveys, focus groups, or panels.
- Specific questions to be answered or information wanted.
- Appropriate questionnaire format, including types of questions (for example: multiple choice, open-ended questions, scaling, and/or ranking alternatives).
- Proper question sequencing.

Figure 8-1. Sample Homeowners Survey

Please use as much room as you need when responding to open end questions. Other questions concerning your home purchasing experience are statements. Your response is to either "agree" or "disagree" with the statement and if you are "uncertain," please mark the appropriate box. Should the statement not apply to your purchasing situation, please mark the "does not apply" box. At the end of the questionnaire, we have asked some questions for classification purposes. You may have previously given us this information; however, we will appreciate the most current information on your household. Please ignore computer tabulation numbers beside the boxes.

1a. Overall, what was the (one) most important reason you selected your home, rather than any other home you may have seen?

_____ (4, 5)

1b. What other reasons did you have for selecting your home?

_____

_____ (6, 7, 8, 9)

SALES PERSON

When you were purchasing your new home...

	Agree	Uncertain	Disagree	Does Not Apply
2. The sales representative was:				
courteous.	☐ 10 · 1	☐ · 2	☐ · 3	☐ · 4
well informed and knowledgeable.	☐ 11 · 1	☐ · 2	☐ · 3	☐ · 4
interested in satisfying my/our housing needs.	☐ 12 · 1	☐ · 2	☐ · 3	☐ · 4
3. The sales representative provided me/us with complete and accurate information on:				
alternative floor plans and exteriors.	☐ 13 · 1	☐ · 2	☐ · 3	☐ · 4
standard features.	☐ 14 · 1	☐ · 2	☐ · 3	☐ · 4
optional features and their costs.	☐ 15 · 1	☐ · 2	☐ · 3	☐ · 4
financing alternatives.	☐ 16 · 1	☐ · 2	☐ · 3	☐ · 4
closing costs.	☐ 17 · 1	☐ · 2	☐ · 3	☐ · 4
anticipated monthly payment.	☐ 18 · 1	☐ · 2	☐ · 3	☐ · 4
mortgage application and processing.	☐ 19 · 1	☐ · 2	☐ · 3	☐ · 4
construction methods and features.	☐ 20 · 1	☐ · 2	☐ · 3	☐ · 4
the location of schools, shopping, recreational, medical and other facilities.	☐ 21 · 1	☐ · 2	☐ · 3	☐ · 4

128

MORTGAGE AND CLOSING

4. My/our mortgage lender was helpful and courteous. 22-1 ☐ ·2 ☐ ·3 ☐ ·4 ☐

5. I/we were fully briefed on what to expect at closing (check amount, closing costs, documents needed, etc.) 23-1 ☐ ·2 ☐ ·3 ☐ ·4 ☐

6a. The closing was a comfortable experience for me/us. 24-1 ☐ ·2 ☐ ·3 ☐ ·4 ☐

6b. *If you are uncertain or disagree, why do you disagree? Please explain.* _____

(25, 26, 27, 28)

CONSTRUCTION

	Agree	Uncertain	Disagree	Does Not Apply
7. During construction, the builder of my/our home was:				
courteous.	29-1 ☐	·2 ☐	·3 ☐	·4 ☐
well informed and knowledgeable.	30-1 ☐	·2 ☐	·3 ☐	·4 ☐
interested in my/our concerns.	31-1 ☐	·2 ☐	·3 ☐	·4 ☐

	Agree	Uncertain	Disagree	Does Not Apply
8. Prior to closing, the ORIENTATION / WALKTHROUGH with the builder included:				
maintenance instructions on my/our new home.	32-1 ☐	·2 ☐	·3 ☐	·4 ☐
an explanation of the operation of appliances and equipment.	33-1 ☐	·2 ☐	·3 ☐	·4 ☐
copies of appliance and equipment warranties.	34-1 ☐	·2 ☐	·3 ☐	·4 ☐
a copy of the ORIENTATION Checklist.	35-1 ☐	·2 ☐	·3 ☐	·4 ☐
written procedures and forms for routine service requests.	36-1 ☐	·2 ☐	·3 ☐	·4 ☐
written procedures for emergency service requests.	37-1 ☐	·2 ☐	·3 ☐	·4 ☐
answers to my/our construction questions.	38-1 ☐	·2 ☐	·3 ☐	·4 ☐

9a. Were all ORIENTATION Checklist items noted and discrepancies completed to your satisfaction, prior to move-in?

39 · 1 ☐ Yes   ·2 ☐ No

129

Figure 8.1. Sample Homeowners Survey (continued)

9b. *If no*, please explain what was not satisfactorily completed. _____

_____ (40, 41, 42, 43)

10. Did our customer service department respond to your service request in an efficient and timely manner?

44 - 1 ☐ Yes   - 2 ☐ No

11a. Based upon your experience to date, is your home's construction: *PLEASE CHECK ONE*

45 - 1 ☐ the best available in its price range?

- 2 ☐ among the best available in its price range?

- 3 ☐ about average compared to other builders' comparably priced homes?

- 4 ☐ not as good as other builders' comparably priced homes?

11b. *If it is about average or not as good*, please explain. _____

_____ (46, 47, 48, 49)

12. Would you recommend Summerhomes to a friend? 50 - 1 ☐ Yes   - 2 ☐ No

13. Is there anything Summerhomes can do to improve its sales presentation?

_____

_____ (51, 52)

14. Do you have any comments concerning the builder of your home? _____

_____ (53, 54)

15. Is there anything Summerhomes can do to improve its construction methods?

_____

_____ (55, 56)

16. Is there anything Summerhomes can do to make the purchase of a home a more pleasant and enjoyable experience?

_____

_____ (57, 58)

THE FOLLOWING QUESTIONS ARE FOR CLASSIFICATION PURPOSES ONLY

17. How many homes have you purchased?

    59 - 1 ☐ This is my/our first home.

    - 2 ☐ This is my/our second or third home.

    - 3 ☐ I/we have purchased three or more homes in the past.

18. What is your marital status?

    60 - 1 ☐ Single   - 3 ☐ Separated

    - 2 ☐ Married   - 4 ☐ Divorced

19. How many people live in your household? _____ (61)

20. What are the approximate ages of the persons in your household over 18 years old?

	First Person	Second Person	Third Person	Fourth Person
18 to 24 years	☐ 62 - 1	☐ 63 - 1	☐ 64 - 1	☐ 65 - 1
25 to 34 years	☐ - 2	☐ - 2	☐ - 2	☐ - 2
35 to 44 years	☐ - 3	☐ - 3	☐ - 3	☐ - 3
45 to 54 years	☐ - 4	☐ - 4	☐ - 4	☐ - 4
55 to 64 years	☐ - 5	☐ - 5	☐ - 5	☐ - 5
65 to 74 years	☐ - 6	☐ - 6	☐ - 6	☐ - 6
75 years old or more	☐ - 7	☐ - 7	☐ - 7	☐ - 7

21. What is your approximate household income annually from all sources?

    66 - 1 ☐ under $25,000   - 4 ☐ $45,000 to $59,999

    - 2 ☐ $25,000 to $34,999   - 5 ☐ $60,000 to $74,999

    - 3 ☐ $35,000 to $44,999   - 6 ☐ $75,000 or more

22. How many wage earners are in the household? _____ (67)

23. What is the company type and occupational position of each wage earner?

	First Wage Earner	Second Wage Earner	Third Wage Earner
Company	_____ (68)	_____ (70)	_____ (72)
Position	_____ (69)	_____ (71)	_____ (73)

131

- Review and pre-test process, with questions asked of an informally selected group of employees or representative consumers.
- Revision and improvement of questionnaires to ensure accuracy prior to distribution.

Competition Owner Survey. This survey is often conducted to provide comparative results with a builder's own purchasers. This survey requires a recent list of purchasers of competitve builders' homes, which can be obtained from real estate data agencies or court records. This competitive survey can be designed identically to the new owner one-year survey described earlier in this chapter.

Prospect Survey. This survey technique can be extremely useful in evaluating product, marketing, and sales performance. This survey must be custom designed according to the specific characteristics of each development and builder, often with professional assistance from a market research organization. It proves particularly useful if conducted in tandem with a survey of recent purchasers, using similar types of questions for comparative analysis.

Exit Survey. Many builders use this simple survey (Figure 8-2) to solicit visitor responses after the sales presentation. A few multiple choice questions can prove immensely useful, particularly in the early stages of a new community. This questionnaire is usually a simplified version of the follow-up survey and can be designed and tabulated at relatively low cost.

Focus Groups. Some builders have found focus groups (or "group interviewing") extremely useful for making decisions on product definition and merchandising for a new community. Focus groups can be done fairly inexpensively by hiring either a marketing research firm or a psychologist trained in group dynamics. The builder provides a list of key topics for the moderator to discuss. The moderator's job is to draw out the participants' opinions and feelings about a product or service, probing below the surface of their initial opinions and ideas when necessary. Because focus groups are not designed to create judgments, a free flow of information from and among participants is essential to success.

Figure 8-2. Sample Exit Survey

- (Community Logo) -

_____
Date

_____ VISITOR SURVEY

Thank you for visiting our community. We would appreciate your response to the following questions to help us improve our reception for future visitors.

	Superior	Average	Poor
1. Was the sales associate who assisted you:			
(a) Enthusiastic and cheerful?	☐	☐	☐
(b) Polite and well-groomed?	☐	☐	☐
(c) Interested in you and your housing needs?	☐	☐	☐
(d) Knowledgeable about all aspects of the community and dwellings?	☐	☐	☐
(e) Successful in providing a clear and well-organized presentation of the community?	☐	☐	☐

Comments: _____

_____

	Superior	Average	Poor
2. What are your reactions to our community?			
(a) Dwelling exterior design?	☐	☐	☐
(b) Construction quality?	☐	☐	☐
(c) Construction materials?	☐	☐	☐
(d) Interior plans?	☐	☐	☐
(e) Dwelling standard features?	☐	☐	☐
(f) Community amenities?	☐	☐	☐
(G) Community location?	☐	☐	☐

Comments: _____

_____

3. Please rate the degree of importance to you of the following amenities and features:

Amenities	Very Important	Important	Not Important
Clubhouse	☐	☐	☐
Tennis Court	☐	☐	☐
24 Hour Security	☐	☐	☐
Swimming Pool	☐	☐	☐
Jogging Trails	☐	☐	☐

Features	Very Important	Important	Not Important
Security System in Dwellings	☐	☐	☐
2 Car Garage	☐	☐	☐
Separate Dwelling Entrances	☐	☐	☐
Upgrade Carpeting	☐	☐	☐
Extra Insulation in Walls & Ceilings	☐	☐	☐
Heat Pump for A/C System	☐	☐	☐
Microwave Oven in Kitchen	☐	☐	☐
Double Pane Windows	☐	☐	☐

What other features and anemities are <u>very important</u> to you? _____

_____

Figure 8-2. Sample Exit Survey (continued)

4. Have you recently purchased a new home within the last year?

   ☐ YES   ☐ NO

5. If YES, what type of home did you purchase?
   - ☐ Single Family Home
   - ☐ A Condominium
   - ☐ A Townhouse
   - ☐ A Patio Home
   - ☐ A Duplex

6. If NO, do you think you might be purchasing a home within the next year or so?

   ☐ YES   ☐ NO

7. Is our community a consideration in your purchase decision?

   ☐ YES   ☐ NO

8. Are there any negative features of our community that would effect your decision to relocate your home/or/make an investment in our community? If there are, we would appreciate your comments below.

   _____
   _____
   _____
   _____

Now, just a few questions for classification purposes.

9. How did you first learn about our community?
   - ☐ Friend/Relative   ☐ Billboard
   - ☐ REALTOR   ☐ TV/Radio
   - ☐ Newspaper   ☐ Other _____
   - ☐ Magazine

10. What is the zip code of your present home?

    ___ ___ ___ ___ ___

11. What is your marital status?
    - ☐ Single
    - ☐ Married
    - ☐ Divorced/Separated/Widowed

12. How many people live in your household? _____

13. How many people in your household fall into the following age groups?

    Children under 18 years _____

    Adults 18 to 34 years _____

    Adults 35 to 49 years _____

    Adults 50 to 64 years _____

    Adults 65 years or more _____

Chapter Nine

Evaluating Sales Performance

Performance evaluation is the final component of the sales process and the crucial final step to regeneration and improvement of the sales system. Effective performance evaluation serves a watchdog function, ensuring an efficient system reaping profitable results for the builder.

At the heart of performance evaluation is the daily, weekly, monthly, and seasonal monitoring of all marketing and sales activities. Overall performance must then be evaluated with respect to planned targets and budgets, as well as unplanned external events. The final results are management information reports containing recommendations—based upon facts—for improving progress toward sales objectives. Figure 9-1 summarizes a performance evaluation system, indicating responsibilities for salespersons, sales management, marketing management, and builder management.

Salespersons and Performance Evaluation

Performance evaluation begins with information collected by salespersons. As illustrated in Figure 9-1, salespersons prepare six information reports for the system. Several of these reports were described in Chapter Three, "Establishing Sales Policies and Procedures." The reports are described below, along with summary notes on their relationship to performance evaluation:

- The prospect card (Figure 3-8) is the essential data base of the Prospect Control System. Whether maintained manually or by computer, prospect information is vital to both marketing and sales performance evaluation.
- The daily sales activity form (Figure 3-11) provides a summary of prospects and purchasers. It extracts key information from prospect

Figure 9-1. Marketing and Sales Performance Evaluation System

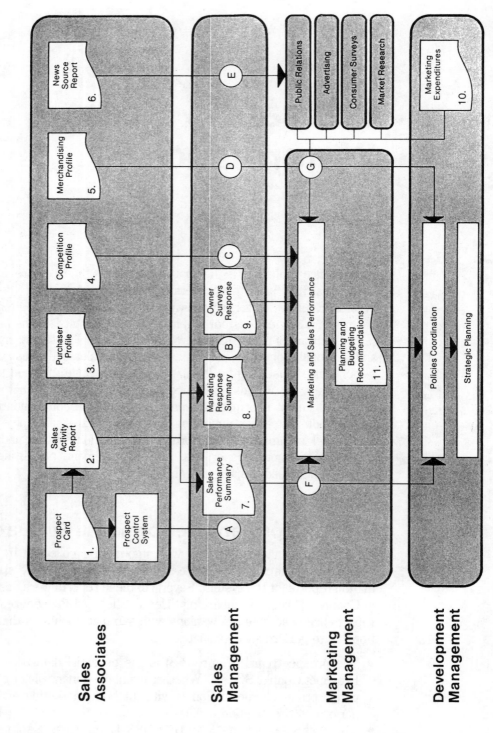

136

cards to a coded format designed as input for marketing and sales performance evaluation.

- The purchaser profile summary (Figure 3-12) generates information on new home purchasers. This report provides origin and source information to compare with prospect data, as well as purchaser characteristics—such as income and household size—to compare with initial product positioning.
- The competition profile compiles relevant information on competitive builder's products, as reported on competitive selling evaluation reports (Figure 3-5).
- The merchandising profile summarizes results from weekly examination of the selling environment, as reported on the weekly merchandising checklist (Figure 3-6).
- The news source report is an informal set of notes (and photographs where available) a salesperson assembles on potentially newsworthy events or activities occurring in a new community: awards, births, special parties, and other events. These news source reports can be transmitted to the builder's public relations agent or directly to news reporters to generate free publicity about the community and/ or the builder's homes. As an additional benefit, community residents often enjoy the publicity.

Although the salesperson's primary mission is to sell new homes, diligent attention to these six information reports will improve marketing and sales support and thereby enhance every salesperson's selling potential.

Computerized Prospect Tracking

An interesting trend among many small-volume builders today is use of a computerized prospect tracking system. With such a system, the builder's sales team can track prospects from initial contact to purchase agreement signing. This system also allows the input of demographic information on each prospect. Several computerized prospect tracking systems are available today, and the smart builder will seek out a system that incorporates tracking of the following elements:

- Media to which the prospect responded.
- Prospect's residential origin, price range, current housing type, preferred model, as well as general prospect quality (graded A, B, C).
- When prospect plans to purchase.
- Broker activity by agency and broker name.
- Activity by salesperson.

This type of information is maintained not only on prospects, but on purchasers as well—resulting in an updated and accurate purchaser profile for the community. Another major benefit of this computerized system is the ease with which the sales director can receive immediate information on the current status of each prospect, either by accessing this information directly through the computer or by reviewing one of the many printouts available through the system.

Sales Management

As illustrated in Figure 9-1, sales management is responsible for generating three reports, as well as monitoring salesperson reporting activities. The three sales management reports are described below:

Sales Activity Summary

The sales activity summary is generated on a weekly or monthly basis from data recorded by salespersons on the daily sales activity report. An increasing number of builders now generate this report by computer in the same format illustrated in Figure 9-2. This report records each salesperson's sales activity in terms of the following:

- new inquiries (TTL and CUM represent total for the period and cumulative for the year or total development period respectively)
- be-backs
- follow-up contacts
- self-prospecting contacts to generate new prospects
- new appointments achieved
- new sales achieved
- cancelled sales
- cumulative sales

The final column calculates sales conversion—cumulative sales divided by cumulative new inquiries. This summary form provides a quick evaluation of each salesperson's performance for the reporting period, as well as a performance check on the entire sales team.

Marketing Response Summary

A marketing response summary (Figure 9-3) provides the basis for comparing the actual results of marketing expenditures with planned objectives. As with the prospect cards described in Chapter Three, origins (place of residence) for new prospect inquiries must be coded according to the geographic and political jurisdiction characteristics of each market area, and the source of each inquiry must be listed according to its origin. Thus, this report provides detailed cross-referencing between sources and origins, in addition to absolute and relative totals for each. This report also records the medium for each inquiry contact: personal site visit, telephone call, or mail inquiry.

Owner Surveys Response Report

The owner surveys response report compiles the results of the owner surveys described in Chapter Eight.

Figure 9-2. Sales Activity Summary

SALES ACTIVITY SUMMARY

Page ___ of ___

Community: ___
Estimated Total Visitor Units: ___
Prepared By: ___ Report Date: ___
Reporting Period: ___
Sales Director: ___

SALES ASSOCIATES	WORK DAYS	NEW INQUIRIES		BE BACKS		FOLLOW UP		PROSPECTING CONTACTS		NEW APPTS		NEW SALES		CANCELLED SALES		CUMULATIVE SALES		SALES CONVER.
#		TTL	CUM	TTL	CUM	TTL	CUM	TTL	CUM	TTL	CUM	NO.	$	NO.	$	NO.	$	
1																		
2																		
3																		
4																		
5																		
6																		
7																		
8																		
9																		
10																		
11																		
12																		
13																		
14																		
15																		
TOTAL																		

Figure 9-3. Marketing Response Summary

Community: _____
Prepared By: _____   Report Date: _____
Reporting Period: _____
Sales Director: _____

Signature

SOURCE CODES	INQUIRY SOURCES	INQUIRY ORIGINS								TOTAL INQUIRIES CUMULATIVE			INQUIRY CONTACTS					
		1	2	3	4	5	6	7	8	TTL	CUM	%	SITE TL	CM	TEL. TL	CM	MAIL TL	CM
BB	Billboard																	
OS	Other Signs																	
NP	Newspapers 1.																	
	2.																	
	3.																	
	4.																	
MG	Magazines																	
TR	Television/Radio																	
DM	Direct Mail																	
PR	Publicity																	
PO	Promotion																	
RF	Referral																	
AR	Agent Referral																	
SP	Self Prospecting																	
SA	Support Advertising																	
RG	Resort Guests																	
	MONTH TOTAL																	

Marketing Management

In addition to information from the above reports, performance evaluation includes gathering current information on such marketing aspects as public relations, advertising, relevant consumer surveys, market research, and actual marketing expenditures for the time period being evaluated.* Thus, as illustrated in Figure 9-4, the cost-effectiveness of various marketing expenditures can be calculated in terms of cost per inquiry.

Clearly, due to the imprecise nature of consumer source reporting, cost-effectiveness calculations must often be modified. For example,

Figure 9-4. Sample Marketing Cost-Effectiveness

	For the Month			Year to Date		
	Inquiries	Cost	Cost/Inquiry	Inquiries	Cost	Cost/Inquiry
Newspapers	42	$13,410	$319.29	388	$72,372	$186.53
Magazines	0	0	NA	0	0	NA
Radio/TV	3	0	0/00	3	991	330.33
Outdoor Signs	102	5,290	51.86	603	33,527	55.60
Direct Mail	0	0	NA	0	0	NA
Support Ads (e.g. Resort)	0	0	NA	0	0	NA
Public Relations	0	1,346	NA	1	6,579	6,579.00
Promotions	0	0	NA	0	0	NA
Referrals	14	0	0.00	129	0	0.00
Agent	35	0	0.00	204	0	0.00
Self-Prospecting	0	0	NA	9	0	0.00
Resort Guest	0	0	NA	0	0	NA
Other Advertising Costs						
Ad Agency Fees	0	3,675	NA	0	22,125	NA
General Advertising	0	2,305	NA	0	10,517	NA
Ad Production	0	275	NA	0	11,817	NA
	196	$23,301	$134.19	1,337	$157,928	$118.12
Other Marketing Costs						
Product Merchandising	0	1,082	NA	0	23,255	NA
Marketing Control	0	2,500	NA	0	15,000	NA
MARKETING TOTAL	196	$29,883	$152.46	1,337	$196,183	$146.73

*See *Marketing New Homes* by Charles R. Clark and David F. Parker (Washington, D.C.: National Association of Home Builders, 1989).

some marketing expenditures, such as public relations, tend to have subliminal rather than direct impact upon consumers. Nevertheless, this comparison of actual marketing expenditures with consumer inquiries does provide a useful arithmetic base that, with the help of good professional judgment, can result in valuable modifications to the marketing and sales plan and budget.

Builder Management

Builder management coordinates marketing, sales, and other management policies through periodic planning and budgeting recommendations. Regular sales performance and marketing reports augment these activities. This supplementary information is essential to decision-making on marketing management's planning and budgeting recommendations. Regardless of how many people are involved in the generation of this information (in a small organization, it might involve only two or three people with overlapping responsibilities), management decisions on strategic planning for future activities can and should be made efficiently and confidently.

Appendix A:

Area Profile

Identify the Principal Benefits of the General Housing Environment

Name of Community _____

I.	**Major Access Routes to Community**	Distance By Car	
	—shortest routes from following locations	Miles	Minutes

1. Commercial Airport: _____

_____

_____ _____ _____

2. Nearest Executive Airport: _____

_____

_____ _____ _____

3. Interstate _____ intersection: _____

_____

_____ _____ _____

4. Railway Station: _____

_____

_____ _____ _____

5. Bus Terminal: _____

_____

_____ _____ _____

6. Downtown (core city): _____

_____

_____ _____ _____

7. Nearest Major Mall: _____

_____

_____   _____   _____

8. Major Recreation Area: _____

_____

_____   _____   _____

II. Schools

—name, location and principal

1. Public Elementary: _____

_____

_____   _____   _____

2. Public Jr. High: _____

_____

_____   _____   _____

3. Public High School: _____

_____

_____   _____   _____

4. Public School Bus: Is pick up necessary? _____ Yes _____ No.

Is bus service provided for all grades? _____ Yes _____ No.

Up to what grade? _____.

Does homeowner pay for this service? _____ Yes _____ No.

Annual cost: $_____.

5. Parochial Elementary: _____

_____

_____   _____   _____

6. Parochial High School: _____

_____

_____   _____   _____

7. Parochial School Bus: Is pick up necessary? _____ Yes _____ No.

Is bus service provided for all grades? _____ Yes _____ No.

Up to what grade? _____.

Does homeowner pay for this service? _____ Yes _____ No.

Annual cost: $_____.

8. Private Elementary: _____

_____

_____   _____   _____

9. Private High School: _____

_____

_____   _____   _____

10. Private School Bus Service? _____ Yes _____ No.

Annual cost: $_____.

11. Nursery School: _____

_____

_____   _____   _____

12. Day Care Center: _____

_____

_____   _____   _____

13. Community College: _____

_____

_____   _____   _____

14. Other Schools: _____

_____

_____   _____   _____

III. Religious Centers

—name, location and minister/priest/rabbi

1. Jewish: _____

_____

_____   _____   _____

2. Protestant: _____

_____

_____   _____   _____

3. Protestant: _____

_____

_____   _____   _____

4. Protestant: _____

_____

_____   _____   _____

5. Protestant: _____

_____

_____   _____   _____

6. Protestant: _____

_____

_____   _____   _____

7. Roman Catholic: _____

_____

_____   _____   _____

8. Other: _____

_____

_____   _____   _____

9. Other: _____

_____

_____   _____   _____

10. If there is predominance of one or several religious groups in immediate area, please list:

_____

_____

_____

IV. Medical Facilities

—name and location

1. Hospital with Emergency Care: _____

_____   _____   _____

2. Other Hospital: _____

_____   _____   _____

3. Nursing Home: _____

_____   _____   _____

| | | Distance By Car | |
| | | Miles | Minutes |

4. Other Nursing Home: _____   _____ _____

5. Medical Clinic: _____   _____ _____

6. Veterinary Clinic: _____   _____ _____

7. Pharmacy: _____   _____ _____

V. Retail Facilities

—name and location

1. Convenience Store: _____   _____ _____

2. Supermarket: _____   _____ _____

3. Commercial Bank: _____   _____ _____

4. Savings and Loan: _____   _____ _____

5. Neighborhood Shopping Center: _____   _____ _____

6. Regional Shopping Center: _____   _____ _____

7. Special Interest Shop(s): _____   _____ _____

VI. Recreation, Social, Cultural Facilities

—name, location, phone number, and fees (if applicable)

1. Movie Theater: _____   _____ _____

2. Bowling Alley: _____   _____ _____

3. Public Golf Course: _____   _____ _____

4. Private Golf Course: _____   _____   _____

5. Public Tennis Courts: _____   _____   _____

6. Private Tennis Club: _____   _____   _____

7. Racquetball Center: _____   _____   _____

8. Public Swimming: _____   _____   _____

9. Private Swim Club: _____   _____   _____

10. Public Park: _____   _____   _____

11. Public Library: _____   _____   _____

12. Live Theater: _____   _____   _____

13. Major Sports Stadium: _____   _____   _____

14. Major Amusement Center: _____   _____   _____

15. Recommended Luncheon Restaurant: _____   _____   _____

16. Recommended Dinner Restaurant: _____   _____   _____

17. Recommended Night Club: _____   _____   _____

VII. Public Facilities

—name, location, phone number, rates (if applicable)

1. City or Township Offices: _____   _____   _____

—Chief elected official: _____

—Type of government: _____
    (e.g. mayor/council, commission, city manager)   _____   _____

2. County Offices: _____

_____   _____   _____

—Chief elected official: _____

—Type of government: _____

3. Local Government Services:

Fire: _____   _____   _____

Police: _____   _____   _____

Ambulance: _____   _____   _____

Garbage Pickup: _____   _____   _____

Water/Sewer: _____   _____   _____

Public Works: _____   _____   _____

Recreation Programs: _____   _____   _____

4. Telephone Company: _____

_____   _____   _____

5. Electric Company: _____

_____   _____   _____

6. Gas Company: _____

_____   _____   _____

7. Cable TV Company: _____

_____   _____   _____

8. Water/Sewer (non-government): _____

_____   _____   _____

9. Private Garbage Collection: _____

_____   _____   _____

10. Other: _____

_____   _____   _____

VIII. Local News Media

—name, cost, phone number

1. Morning Daily Paper: _____
2. Evening Daily Paper: _____
3. Area Weekly Papers: _____
4. Area Magazines: _____

_____

IX. Local Groups, Clubs, Organizations

—location, phone number, contact person

1. YM/YWCA: _____   _____   _____
2. YMHA: _____   _____   _____
3. Cub Scouts: _____   _____   _____
4. Boy Scouts: _____   _____   _____
5. Brownies: _____   _____   _____
6. Girl Scouts: _____   _____   _____
7. Little League: _____   _____   _____
8. American Legion: _____   _____   _____
9. VFW: _____   _____   _____
10. JWV: _____   _____   _____
11. Cath. Vet.: _____   _____   _____
12. Chamber of Commerce: _____   _____   _____
13. Jaycees: _____   _____   _____
14. Rotary: _____   _____   _____
15. Kiwanis: _____   _____   _____
16. Lions: _____   _____   _____
17. Elks: _____   _____   _____
18. Masons: _____   _____   _____
19. K of C: _____   _____   _____
20. K of P: _____   _____   _____
21. Others: _____   _____   _____

X. Local Public Transportation

—name, nearest stop or location, frequency

1. Bus: _____

   _____

   _____

2. Commuter or Express Bus: _____

   _____

   _____

3. Commuter Train: _____

   _____

   _____

4. Taxis: _____

   _____

   _____

AREA: _____

TOP 10 MOST IMPORTANT

ADVANTAGES	DISADVANTAGES

Appendix B:

Product Profile

The Benefits of Living in Your Home

Name of Community: _____

I.   **Exterior Features:** _____

       _____

       _____

       _____

II.   **Interior Features:**

    1. Entry Foyer: _____

        _____

        _____

    2. Living Area: _____

        _____

        _____

    3. Dining Area: _____

        _____

        _____

    4. Kitchen Area: _____

        _____

        _____

5. Owner's Bedroom Suite (1): _____

   _____

   _____

6. Bedroom (2): _____

   _____

   _____

7. Bedroom (3): _____

   _____

   _____

8. Bedroom (4): _____

   _____

   _____

9. Owner's Bath and Dressing Area: _____

   _____

   _____

10. Bathroom (2): _____

    _____

    _____

11. Bathroom (3): _____

    _____

    _____

12. Washroom: _____

    _____

    _____

13. Den/Sitting Area or Loft: _____

    _____

    _____

14. Utility Area: _____

    _____

    _____

15. Balconies/Decks/Patios: _____

    _____

    _____

16. Garage, Carport, Parking: _____

_____

_____

17. Exterior Storage: _____

_____

_____

III. Optional "Extras"

Please list below the standard optional extras that will be offered in all models:

_____ _____ _____

_____ _____ _____

_____ _____ _____

IV. Decorating Choices

What choices in decorating effects will buyers make themselves? Please list (e.g. exterior color, paint, woods, tile, etc.) the number of colors or choices available in each category:

_____ _____ _____

_____ _____ _____

_____ _____ _____

V. Construction Methods and Details

Are there any unusual construction methods used that can be translated into consumer benefits?

_____ Yes _____ No

If Yes, please describe briefly: _____

_____

_____

VI. Negative Features

List and describe any negative features about the product: _____

_____

_____

VII. Financial Data

1. What type of financing for the homeowner does the builder offer?

_____ F.H.A. _____ V.A. _____ Conventional

Creative financing programs (describe): _____

_____

2. Minimum deposit required: _____

3. Applicable insurance: Monthly premium: $ _____ to $ _____

4. Are closing costs absorbed in price of home? _____ Yes _____ No
   If no, please check off what they cover:

   _____ Certificate of Title   _____ Tax Escrow _____Years

   _____ Recording Fees   _____ Amortization Schedule

   _____ Mortgage Title Insurance   _____ Homeowner's Insurance
            Policy   Policy

   _____ Spot Land Survey   _____ Service Charges

   _____ Appraisal on Land   _____ Other _____

5. Lowest total monthly investment—include principal, interest, amortization, taxes, and homeowner's insurance

   policy: $ _____

6. Highest total monthly investment: $ _____

7. Money required to hold lot (deposit or binder): $ _____

8. Money required to go to Purchase and Sale Agreement:

   $ _____–_____ %

9. What is the approximate cost for closing? $ _____

10. What type of annual income is necessary to purchase the home?

   $ _____

VIII. What Type of Prospect Are You Looking For?

Please describe with relation to education; family accumulation; age; first, second, third homeowner; etc: _____

_____

_____

_____

_____

_____

_____

_____

_____

_____

_____

_____

_____

Glossary

Applicant pool. A group of qualified persons for a specific employment position from which an employer may choose to hire.

Benefits. All forms of compensation other than salary and/or commission, including, but not limited to, vacation time, sick leave, health insurance, and company car.

Be-back. Designation assigned to a prospect who returns to visit a community or model home.

Board of REALTORS®. A trade association providing a variety of services to real estate brokers, chartered by the National Association of REALTORS® on a state and local basis.

Broker cooperation. The association of a real estate broker or agent with a builder's new homes sales staff for the mutual benefit of achieving a sale, usually entailing the payment of commission to the participating broker in addition to the relevant new homes salesperson.

Budget method of determining number of salespersons. This method includes the division of typical salesperson earnings into the projected revenues for a development in order to calculate an adequate sales force.

Commission arbitration. The hearing and determination of the handling of a commission in controversy, usually by the local Board of REALTORS®.

Compensation agreement. An agreement (preferably signed) between employer and salesperson/sales director that outlines in detail every element of the compensation program offered.

Competition organizer. Typically a three-ring binder containing up-to-date product and selling information on competitive products: brochures, prices, financing plans, etc.

Competition owner survey. Survey of competitor's owners conducted to provide comparative results with a particular builder's owners.

Conversion rate. A comparison of new sales versus new prospect inquiries. For example, a salesperson who achieves one sale for every twenty prospects achieves a 5 percent conversion rate.

Convertibility. The potential for conversion of a builder's prospect to purchase another home offered by a cooperating broker on the assumption that the cooperating broker will reciprocate in the future with a purchaser discovered through another source.

Critical Path to Successful Selling. A series of activities and events designed to take a prospect from the initial greeting to signing of the purchase agreement, all occurring within the four phases of **Introduction, Demonstration, Finalization,** and **Continuation.**

Direct mail. A form of advertising involving the mailing of a professionally prepared flyer or marketing brochure to a defined target group.

Effectiveness. In the context of new home sales, a comparison of net sales against individual goals.

Exit survey. A questionnaire used to gather opinions from visitors to a model center or home immediately upon completion of their visit.

Focus groups. A form of market research whereby a market research firm or specially trained psychologist conducts group interviews of selected participants to determine opinions and feelings about a series of topics, usually pre-defined by the builder.

Follow-up contacts. Any type of contact made with a prospect following the initial visit, either in person, over the telephone, or by mail.

Full-time employee. An employee who receives benefits and for whom all required state and federal taxes are withheld by the employer.

General broker contact list. An extensive list of brokers developed without regard to specific qualifications of the firms or individuals identified.

Good Neighbor Program. A program that concentrates on owner referral generation through improved purchaser satisfaction.

High achiever contact list. A list of brokers that specifically identifies top-producing firms and brokers.

In-house cooperation. Two (or more) in-house salespersons working in concert with one prospect, which may include a split sales commission once the sale is made.

In-house sales team. Sales director and salespersons who work solely for the builder and sell only the builder's products.

M.I.R.M. Designation assigned to all members of the Institute of Residential Marketing, established within the National Sales and Marketing Council of the National Association of Home Builders.

New inquiries. All first-time visitors to a community or site who are identified as prospects (by name, address, etc.).

New licensee contact list. A list of recent real estate licensees who can be targeted for new home sales training or other forms of special promotion.

New owner survey program. A program surveying all purchasers regarding their needs, levels of satisfaction, product features and designs, marketing effectiveness, and sales presentation. Purchasers are usually surveyed the first few weeks after purchase, and again after one year.

Operations policies. General working agreement that provides direction for individual and team performance and is subject to modification in accordance with changing needs and requirements.

Orientation. An new employee's introduction to the company, sales environment and procedures, product, community, and competition.

Perceived value. The prospect's assessment of product and community quality, based primarily upon subjective perception rather than specific objective considerations.

Performance evaluation system. A tracking system (including the prospect card and daily sales activity report) used to determine the effectiveness of all marketing and selling efforts.

Product orientation. Full employee familiarization with all builder products in terms of price, size, features, and benefits.

Production. In the context of new home sales, a ratio based upon the number of prospect contacts and the extent of selling time.

Prospect. A potential purchaser of a home who has indicated at least minimal interest and who is known to the sales staff in terms of name, address, and telephone number.

Prospect card. Card used to maintain specific information (for example, name, address, price range, buying timeframe) on each prospect visiting a model home or community.

Prospect follow-up system. A system established to ensure that prospect registration is followed up in a systematic fashion for the end result of improving the number of be-backs.

Prospect survey. A questionnaire that evaluates product, marketing, and sales performance perceptions, usually through a mail-in format sent to prospects two weeks after the initial visit.

Prospecting. Actions taken by salespersons to generate further new inquiries and stimulate consumer interest.

Purchaser satisfaction program. Services provided through a series of events designed to ensure that a purchaser remains satisfied with his or her purchase.

Rapid response mailing. A follow-up technique consisting of one of three types of mailings: direct mail, personal notes, and collateral information.

Referral prospect. A prospect referred to a community, model home, or site through word of mouth.

Retainage. That portion of a sales commission retained by the company for purchase agreements not closed at the time of employment termination.

Return and forfeiture of deposit. Purchase deposits that are either returned to the prospect or forfeited due to a purchase agreement cancellation, requiring fully defined policies for proper handling.

Salesperson. A professional whose primary mission is to correctly and effectively present community, product, and builder to consumers in order to sell property.

Sales Director. A professional who provides management and leadership for planning, directing, and implementing the company's sales policies, strategies, and programs to achieve company sales volume goals.

Sales organizer. Typically a three-ring binder including all documents, floor plans, prices, options, pertinent memos, and other information for quick reference by salespersons.

Sales policies and procedures manual. A document defining all company policies and procedures.

Settlement procedures. Procedures established for use at all purchase agreement closing meetings.

Subjective method of determining number of salespersons. This method is based upon prior experience rather than a methodical examination of projected revenues and average salesperson compensation within the area.

Success zone. An optimum period of time spent with a prospect, which varies depending upon the communications medium.

Support staff. Employees who provide receptionist and secretarial assistance to salespersons when warranted by traffic volume.

Termination agreement. A signed agreement outlining the procedure used for commissions on sales not closed at the time of employee termination.

Walk-in traffic. Term applied to prospects visiting a community or model home who simply "happen to stop by" rather that directly responding to advertising or promotional activities. Also referred to a "drive-by traffic."